My Fun Book of Questions and Answers

Miles Kelly

First published in 2017 by Miles Kelly Publishing Ltd
Harding's Barn, Bardfield End Green, Thaxted, Essex, CM6 3PX, UK

Copyright © Miles Kelly Publishing Ltd 2017

This edition published 2020

4 6 8 10 9 7 5

Publishing Director Belinda Gallagher
Creative Director Jo Cowan
Editors Carly Blake, Sarah Carpenter, Becky Miles, Claire Philip
Designers Fineline Studios, Rob Hale, Joe Jones, Sally Lace
Production Elizabeth Collins, Jennifer Brunwin-Jones
Image Manager Liberty Newton
Reprographics Stephan Davis
Assets Lorraine King

All rights reserved. No part of this publication may be reproduced, stored in a retrieval system, or transmitted by any means, electronic, mechanical, photocopying, recording or otherwise, without the prior permission of the copyright holder.

ISBN 978-1-78989-059-4

Printed in China

British Library Cataloguing-in-Publication Data
A catalogue record for this book is available from the British Library

Made with paper from a sustainable forest

www.mileskelly.net

Contents

Science 4
Human Body 34
Planet Earth 64
Oceans 102
Plants 132
Seashore 162
Rainforests 192
Coral Reef 222
Big Cats 252
Baby Animals 282
Monkeys and Apes 312
Deadly Creatures 342
Index 372

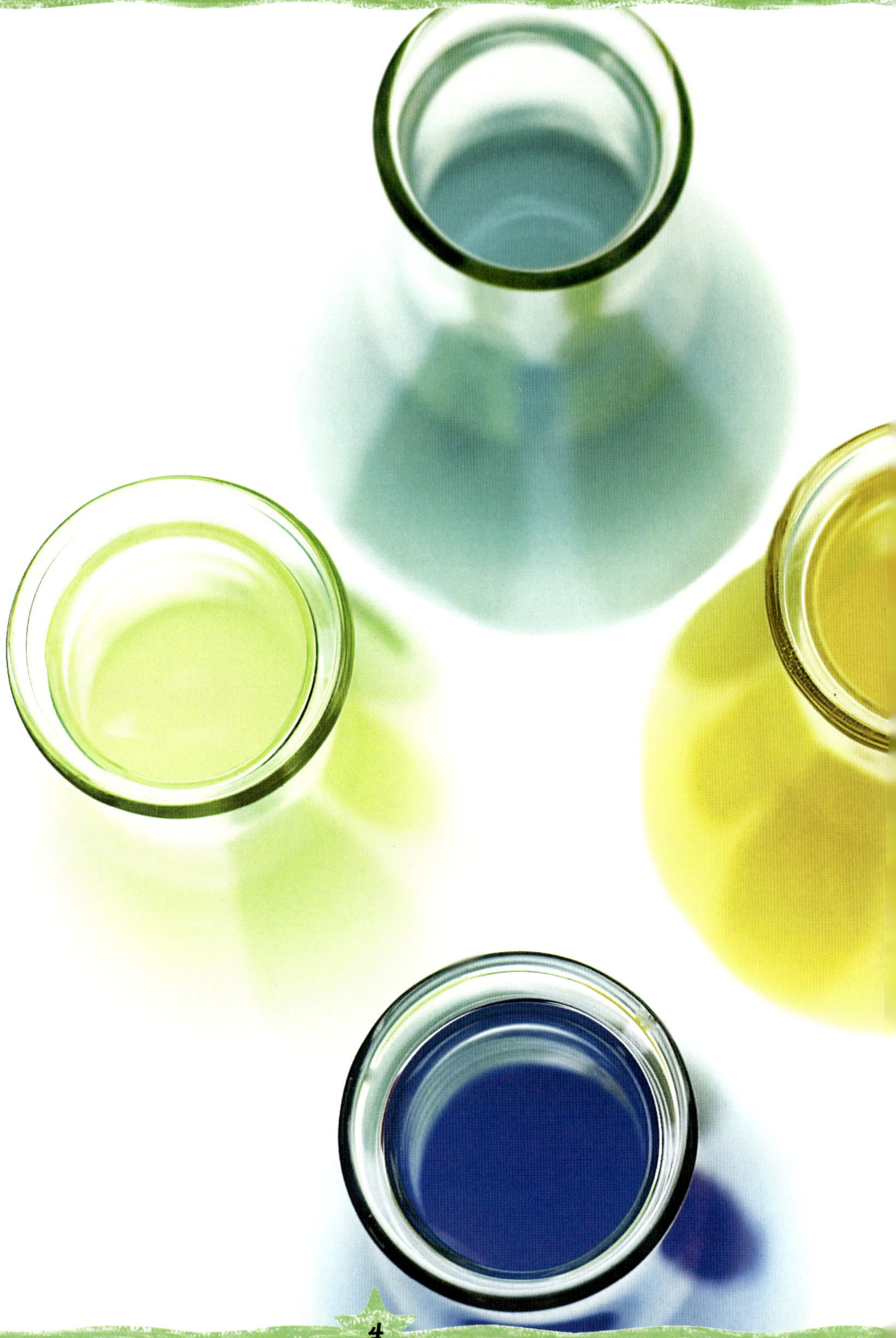

Science

Is science in the playground?

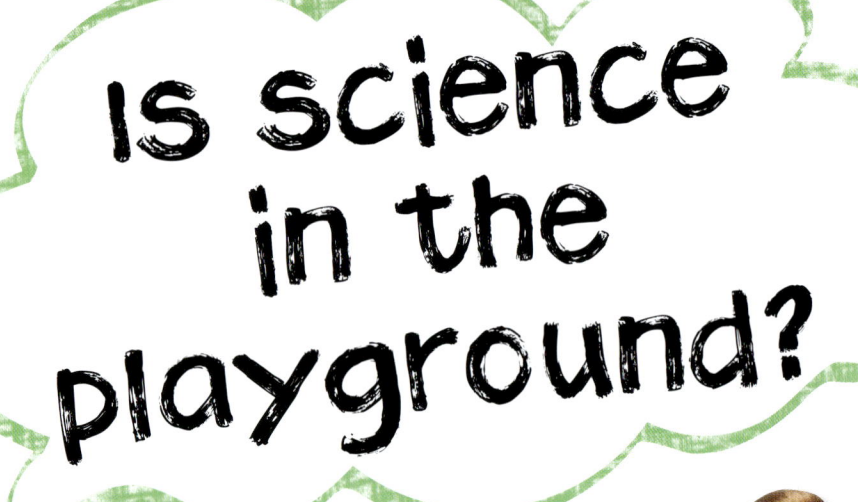

Yes, it is! Lots of science happens in a playground. The playground rides could not work without science. A see-saw is a simple machine called a lever. It has a long arm and a point in the middle called a pivot. As you ride on the see-saw, the lever tips up and down on the pivot.

Lever

Pivot

See-saw

Feel
Press your palm onto a table. A force called friction stops you sliding your hand along.

What is a wheel?

Riding bikes

A wheel is a very simple machine that can spin around. Wheels let other machines, such as skateboards, bicycles, cars and trains, roll along smoothly. They also make it easy to move heavy weights in carts and wheelbarrows.

Sloping machine

A ramp is the simplest machine of all. It is easier to walk up a ramp to the top of a hill than it is to climb a steep hillside.

What makes things stop and start?

Pushes and pulls make things stop and start. Scientists use the word 'force' for pushes and pulls. Forces are all around us. The force of gravity pulls things downwards. It makes a rollercoaster car hurtle downhill. It also slows the car on the uphill parts of the track.

Rollercoaster

Why do fireworks flash and bang?

Fireworks flash and bang because they are full of chemicals that burn. The chemicals have lots of energy stored in them. When they burn, the energy changes to light, heat and sound. We use chemicals that burn in other places too, such as cookers, heaters and car engines.

Fireworks

How do candles burn?

Candles are made of wax and a wick (string). When the wick is lit, the wax around it melts. The wick then soaks up the liquid wax and the heat of the flame turns the wax into a gas (vapour), which burns away. As the wax becomes vapour it cools the wick, allowing the candle to burn slowly.

Candles

Hot! Hot! Hot!
The hottest-ever temperature recorded was in a science laboratory. It was four hundred million degrees Celsius (400,000,000°C).

Remember
Which piece of equipment is used to measure how hot or cold something is?

Thermometer

What is a thermometer?

A thermometer is an instrument that tells us how hot something is. This is called temperature. The numbers on a thermometer are normally degrees Celsius (°C). If you put a thermometer in cold water, it shows 0°C. If you put it in boiling water it shows 100°C. A thermometer can also measure body temperature.

How does light bend?

Light rays travel in straight lines. When light shines through a prism, the rays bend because light travels more slowly through glass than air. Sunlight is called white light, but it is made up of a mixture of colours. When white light passes through a prism it splits into many colours, like a rainbow.

Make
On a sunny day, stand with your back to the Sun. Spray water into the air and you should see a rainbow!

White light

Prism (glass triangle)

Fast as light
Light is the fastest thing in the Universe. It travels 300,000 kilometres every second. That means it could travel around the Earth seven times in less than a second!

What is the loudest sound?

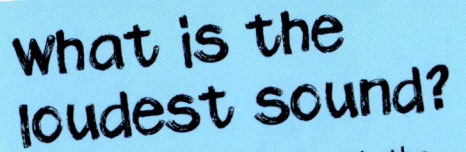

The roar of a jet engine is the loudest sound we normally hear. It is thousands of times louder than someone shouting. Sounds this loud can damage our ears if we are too close to them.

Jet aircraft

Rainbow colours

Battery

Wires

Electricity flows along wires

Magnet on side of motor

Spindle

What is inside an electric motor?

Magnets and wires are inside an electric motor. Electricity from a battery passes through the wires, which turns the wires into a magnet. Two more magnets on each side of the motor push and pull against the wires. This makes a thin metal rod (spindle) spin around.

where is science in a city?

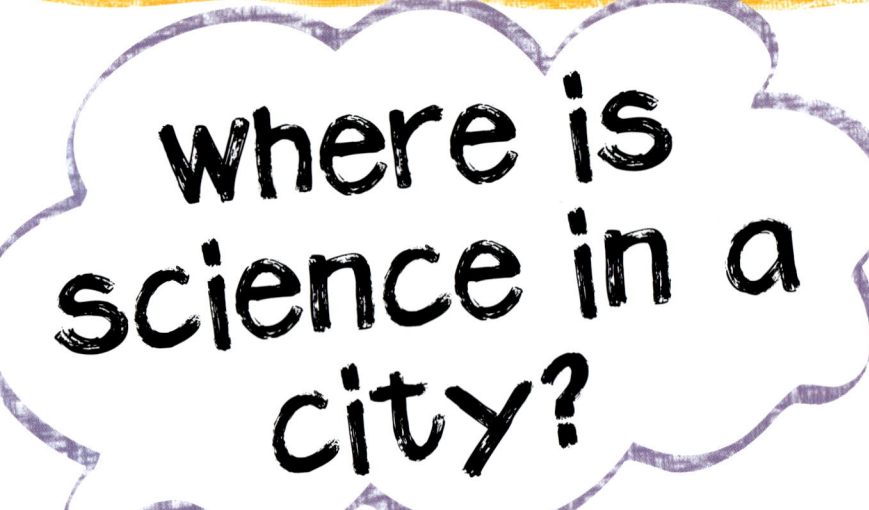

Everywhere! In a big city, almost every machine, building and vehicle is based on science. Cars, buses and trains help us move around the city. Scientists and engineers have also worked out how to build tall skyscrapers where people live and work.

City

Spot
Look at this city picture. How many different forms of transport can you spot?

Railway signals

Who works railway signals?

Nobody does – the signals work by themselves. Electronic parts on the track work out if a train is passing. Then a computer changes the signals to red, to stop another train moving onto the same piece of track.

How do skyscrapers stay up?

Skyscrapers stay up because they have a strong frame on the inside. The frame is made from steel and concrete. These are very strong materials. Normally you can't see the frame. It is hidden by the skyscraper's walls. The walls hang on the frame.

Plane spotters

There's science at an airport, too. A radar machine uses radio waves to find aircraft in the sky. This helps people at the airport to guide the aircraft onto the runway.

Skyscrapers

How do you make magnets?

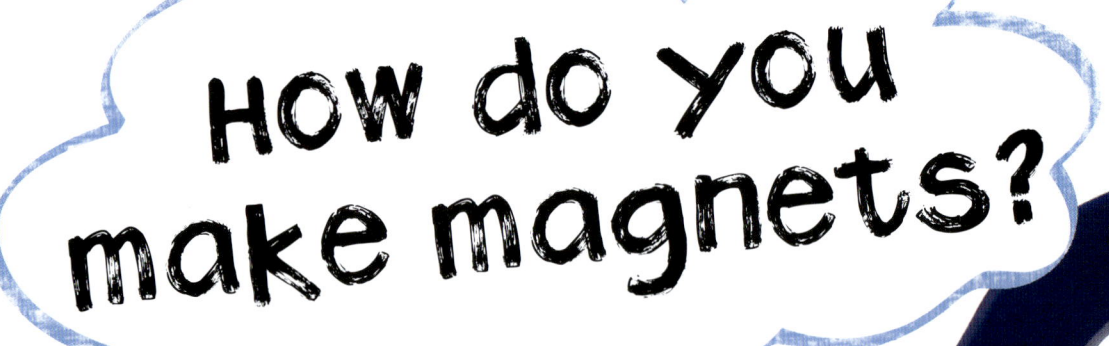

By using another magnet. Magnets are made from lumps of iron or steel. You can turn a piece of iron into a magnet by stroking it with another magnet. A magnet can also be made by sending electricity through a coil of wire. This is called an electromagnet. Some electromagnets are so strong, they can pick up cars.

Magnet

count
Find a magnet at home (you can use a fridge magnet). How many paper clips can your magnet pick up?

Does a magnet have a field?

Yes – but it's not a field of grass. The area around a magnet is called a magnetic field. A magnetic field is shown by drawing lines around a magnet. The Earth has a magnetic field, too. It is as though there is a giant magnet inside the Earth.

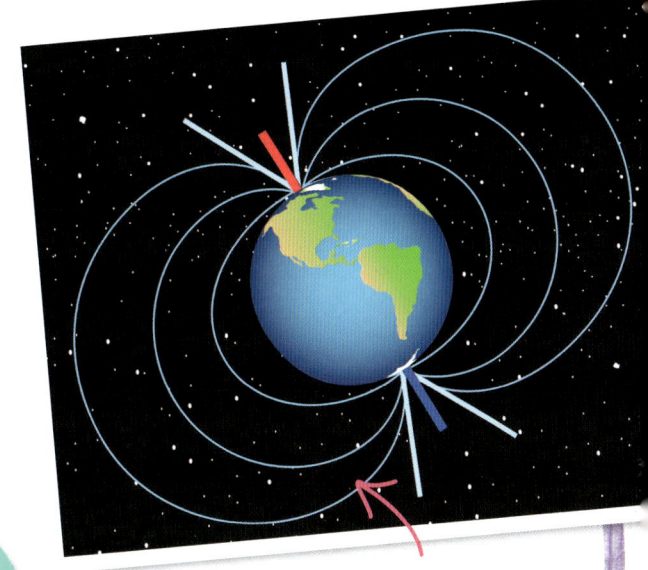

Magnetic field

Handy rock

Some rocks act like magnets. Years ago, people used magnetic rocks to find their way. If they let the rock spin round, it always pointed in the same direction.

What are poles?

Every magnet has two poles. These are where the pull of a magnet is strongest. They are called the north pole and the south pole. A north pole and a south pole always pull towards each other. Two north poles always push each other away. So do two south poles.

15

where does electricity come from?

Electricity comes to your home along cables from power stations. The cables are held off the ground by pylons. Around your home are holes in the wall called sockets. When a machine is plugged into a socket, electricity flows out to work the machine.

Excellent electric

Our homes are full of machines that use a lot of electricity. If we didn't have access to electricity we wouldn't have televisions, lights, washing machines or computers!

Power station

Pylon holds cables off the ground

Lightning

When is electricity in the sky?

When there's a thunderstorm. During a storm, a kind of electricity called static electricity builds up, which can make a big flash, that lights up the sky. This is lightning. The hot lightning heats up the air around it, which makes a loud clap. This is thunder.

What is a circuit?

A circuit is a loop that electricity moves around. This circuit is made up of a battery, a light bulb and a switch. If the switch is turned off, the loop would be broken. Then the electricity would stop moving and the light would go out.

Battery

Light bulb

Switch

Remember
Mains electricity is dangerous. It could kill you. Never play with sockets in your home.

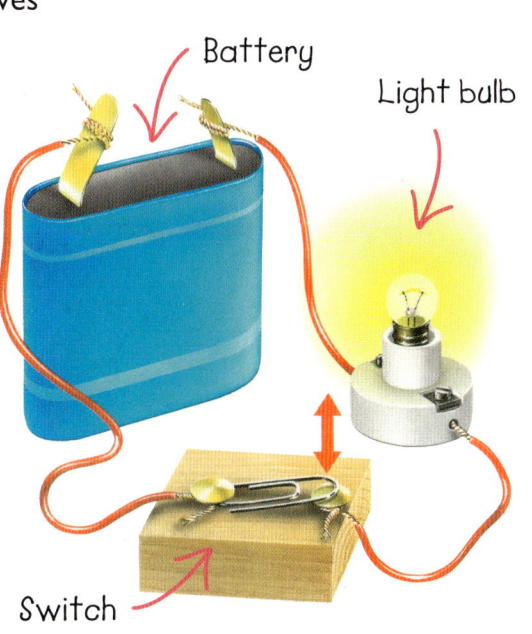

What waves are invisible?

Satellite

Radio waves are all around us, but we can't see them. We use radio waves to send sounds and pictures to radios and televisions. Some radio waves come from satellites in space. A radio set receives radio waves through a metal rod called an aerial. A dish-shaped aerial picks up radio waves for television programmes.

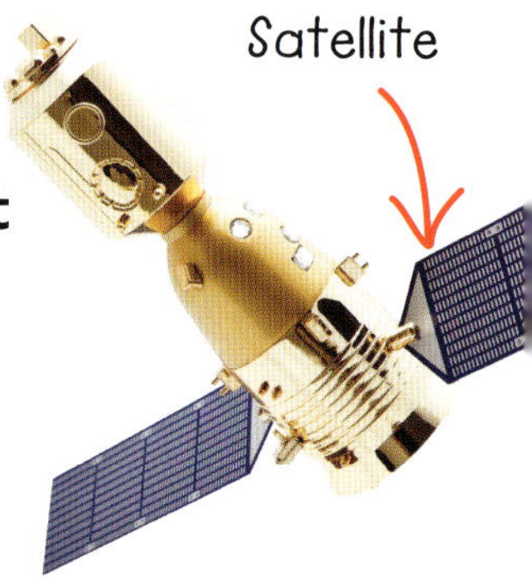

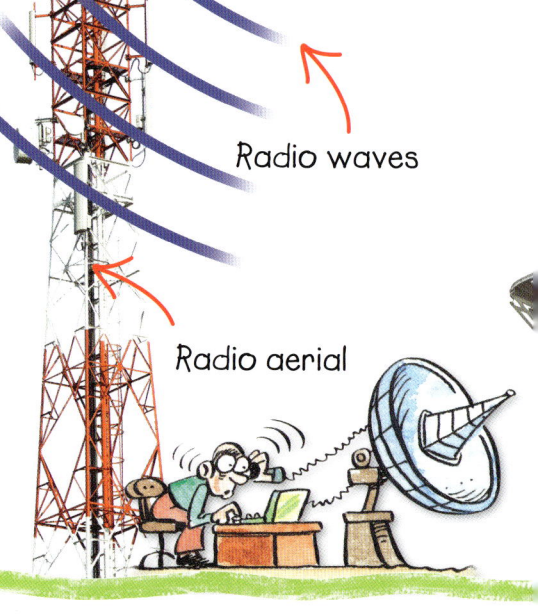

Radio waves

Radio aerial

Space radio

Radio waves can travel through space. But they can't travel through water. So you can listen to a radio in a space station, but not in a submarine!

What is an X-ray?

An X-ray is like a radio wave. X-rays can go through the soft bits of your body. However, hard bones stop them. That's why doctors use X-ray machines to take pictures of the inside of people's bodies.

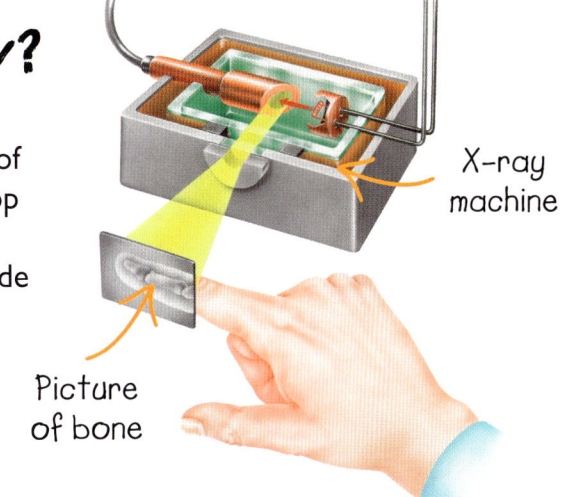

X-ray machine

Picture of bone

Remember
Which part of your body would stop an X-ray? Skin or bone?

What waves can cook food?

Microwaves can. These are a kind of radio wave. They have lots of energy in them. A microwave uses this energy to cook food. Microwaves are fired into the oven. They make the particles in the food jiggle about. This makes the food hot.

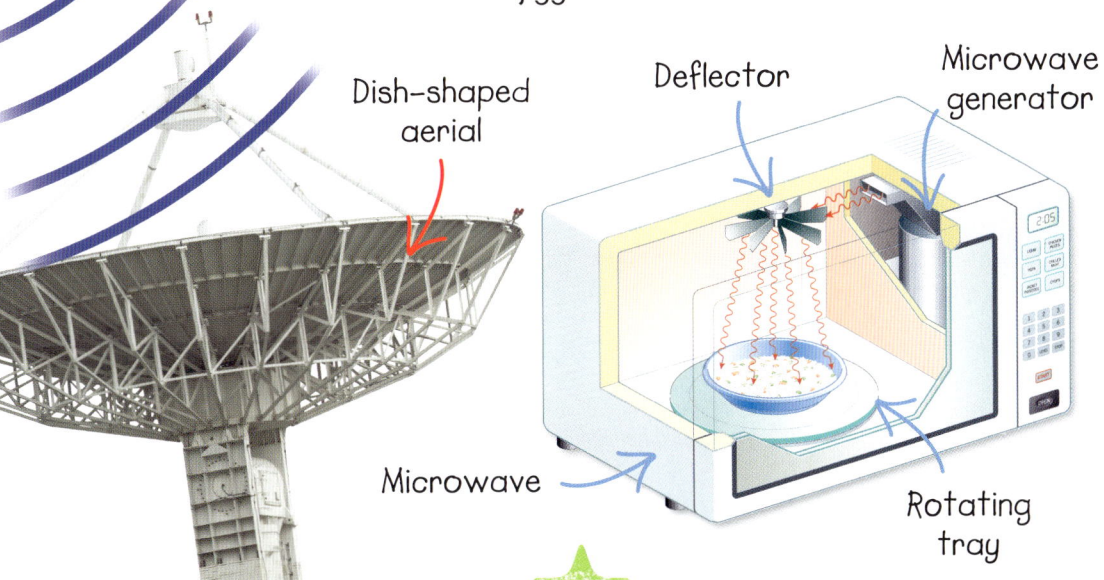

Dish-shaped aerial

Deflector

Microwave generator

Microwave

Rotating tray

Are computers clever?

Not really. Computers are amazing machines, but they can only do what they are told. They carry out computer programs written by people. These are full of instructions that the computer follows. You can also tell a computer what to do by using its keyboard and mouse.

Screen

Laptop

Keyboard

Read
What is the name of a computer's electronic brain? Read these pages again to help you find out.

Microchip

Close-up of microchip

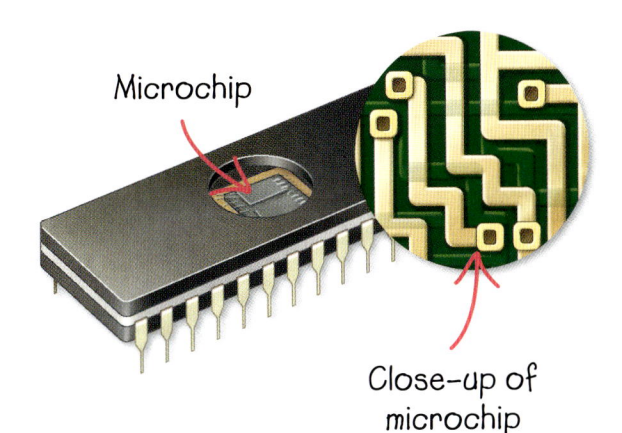

Does a computer have a brain?

A computer doesn't have a brain like yours. It has an electronic brain called a central processing unit. This is a microchip the size of your fingernail, and it can do millions of difficult calculations in a split second.

How does a computer remember?

A computer remembers with its electronic memory made up of microchips. Random Access Memory (RAM) is like a jotting pad and changes as the computer carries out its tasks. Read Only Memory (ROM) is like an instruction book for how all the microchips work together.

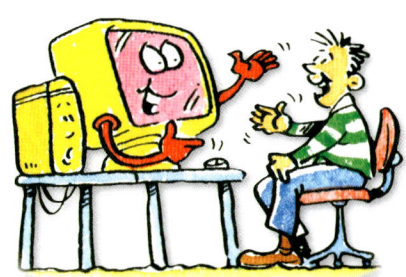

Mouse pad

Computer room

The first computer was made 70 years ago. It was so big that it filled a whole room and weighed almost 50 tonnes.

How is the internet like a web?

The Internet is made up of millions of computers around the world. They are connected like a giant spider's web! A computer connects to a machine called a modem. This sends signals to a server. The server lets you connect to the Internet. People can send emails and open web pages.

Find out
Use the Internet, with a grown-up, to find out who invented the World Wide Web.

What does www stand for?

The letters www are short for World Wide Web. The World Wide Web is like a giant library of information, stored on computers all over the world. There are also thousands of shops on the World Wide Web, where you can buy almost anything.

The world is connected by the Internet

Can I use the Internet without a computer?

Yes. Other machines like mobile phones can link to the Internet, so you can find out information and send and receive emails too. A mobile phone connects to the Internet by radio.

Smartphone

Plenty of pages

The World Wide Web has more than 8000 million pages of information. That's two pages for every person on the planet!

Web page

Can a car be made from card?

Yes, it can – but it would break if you sat inside it! It is always important to use the right material to make something. Cars are made from tough, long-lasting materials, like metal, plastic and rubber.

Think
Can you think of other materials from which things are made? If you get stuck, ask a grown-up.

A racing car is made up of hundreds of parts and different materials

What materials grow?

Many of the materials we use every day come from plants. Wood comes from the trunks and branches of trees. Cotton is made from the seeds of cotton plants to make clothes such as T-shirts. Some rubber is made from a liquid (sap) from rubber trees.

Cotton plants make clothes

Rubber trees make tyres

Tree trunks and branches make wooden bats

Does glass grow?

Glass doesn't grow. It is made from sand and two other materials called limestone and soda. These materials are mixed together and melted to make a gooey liquid. When the mixture cools down, it forms the hard glass that we use to make windows, drinking glasses and other objects.

Bullet proof

Some glass is extra-strong. Toughened glass is so hard that even a bullet from a gun bounces off it!

what do scientists do at work?

Some scientists try to find out about the world around us. Others find out about space, planets and stars. Some scientists discover useful materials that we can use. Scientists carry out experiments in laboratories to test their ideas.

Scientists in a laboratory

Who is the most famous scientist?

The most famous scientist is called Albert Einstein (1879–1955). He made many discoveries about time, space, the force of gravity and nuclear energy. The ideas that Einstein wrote down were so amazing that they made him famous across the world.

Albert Einstein

Find
Where was Albert Einstein born? Can you find out? Use an encyclopedia or the Internet to help you.

Atom pie
One hundred years ago, scientists thought that the tiny pieces in an atom were all spread out, like raisins in a pudding. Now we know they are all bunched together.

Do scientists help doctors?

Yes, they do. Many scientists make medicines that the doctor gives you when you are ill. They also help to make the complicated machines that doctors use in hospitals. Scientists also try to find out what makes us ill, and how we can stay healthy.

Are animals part of science?

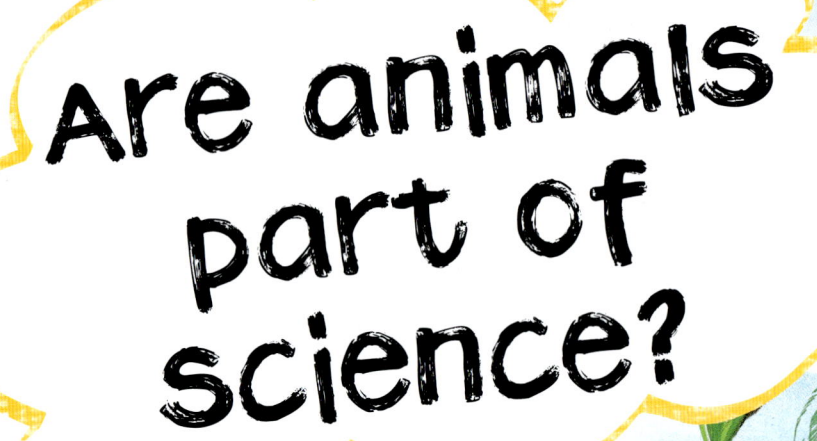

Yes, they are. Scientists who study animals and plants work everywhere in the world. They study in hot rainforests, dusty deserts, high mountains, at the freezing poles and in rivers and seas.

Ecologists study animals and plants

LOOK
Study the picture. Can you see something that might harm the animals and plants?

Which way?

Some animals travel great distances around the world. They use the Earth's magnetic field to guide them.

What is an ecologist?

An ecologist is a scientist. Ecologists study where plants and animals live. They also look at how plants and animals live alongside each other, and the things that animals eat. Ecologists also study the harm that we do to animals.

How do ecologists follow animals?

Radio tag

With complicated radio equipment. First they catch the animal and put a collar on its neck, wing or leg. The collar has a tiny radio aerial that sends out radio waves. The ecologist finds the animal by listening with a machine that picks up the radio waves.

Are we harming the Earth?

Many of the things we do are harming the world around us. Machines such as cars put dangerous gases into the air. These gases can harm plants and make people ill. They are also making the weather change. Scientists are looking for new ways to reduce damage to the Earth.

Pollution

Dirty cars

Cars and other vehicles can produce so much pollution that in some cities it has become difficult for people to breathe.

30

What is recycling?

Recycling is using materials again, instead of throwing them away. This helps to make less waste and reduces the use of raw materials. Glass, paper, metal and plastic can all be recycled and turned into new products.

Recycling

Does electricity harm the Earth?

Yes, it does. Lots of coal, oil and gas are burned to make electricity. These make harmful gases that go into the air. You can help by turning things off to save electricity. Scientists are inventing new ways of making electricity from the wind, the Sun and water.

Save

Ask your family to save electricity. Get them to switch off the lights when nobody is in the room.

Quiz time

3. What is a thermometer?

page 9

Do you remember what you have read about science? These questions will test your memory. The pictures will help you. If you get stuck, read the pages again.

1. Is science in the playground?

page 6

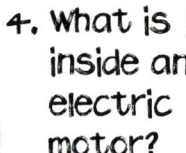

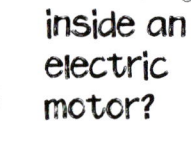

4. What is inside an electric motor?

page 11

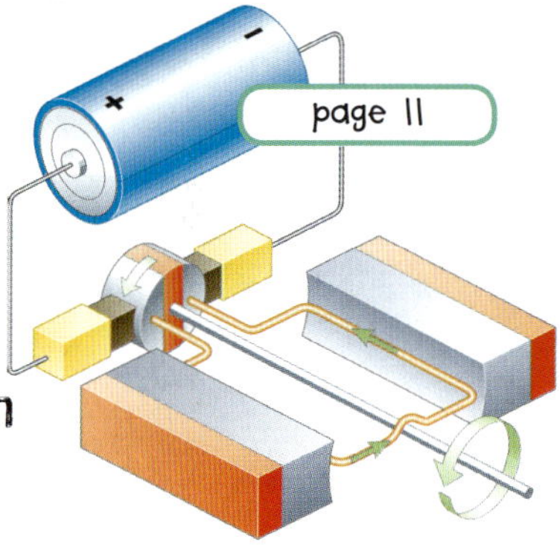

5. How do skyscrapers stay up?

page 13

2. How do candles burn?

page 9

6. Does a magnet have a field?

page 15

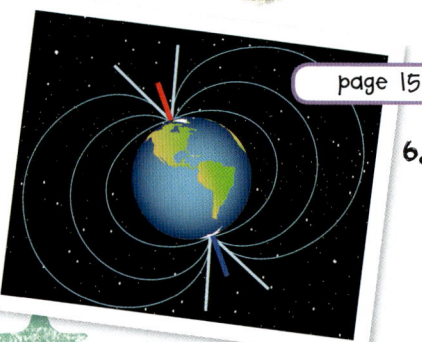

32

7. What are poles?

page 15

page 22

11. What does www stand for?

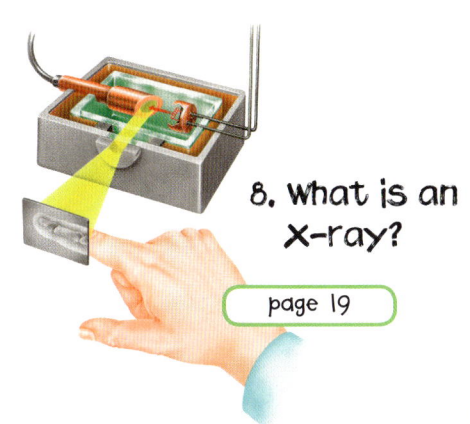

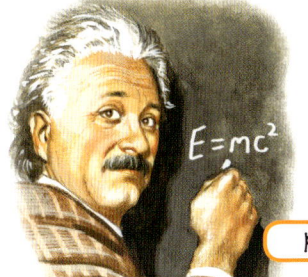

8. What is an X-ray?

page 19

12. Who is the most famous scientist?

page 27

13. Does electricity harm the Earth?

page 31

page 20

9. Are computers clever?

page 21

10. Does a computer have a brain?

Answers

1. Yes it is, in rides such as see-saws
2. By melting wax, which becomes a vapour that burns
3. Something that measures heat
4. Magnets and wires
5. They have a strong frame that supports them
6. Yes, a magnetic field
7. Poles are where the pull of a magnet is strongest
8. It is like a radio wave
9. Not really, but they can carry out complicated programs of instruction
10. It has an electronic brain
11. World Wide Web
12. Albert Einstein
13. Yes, it can

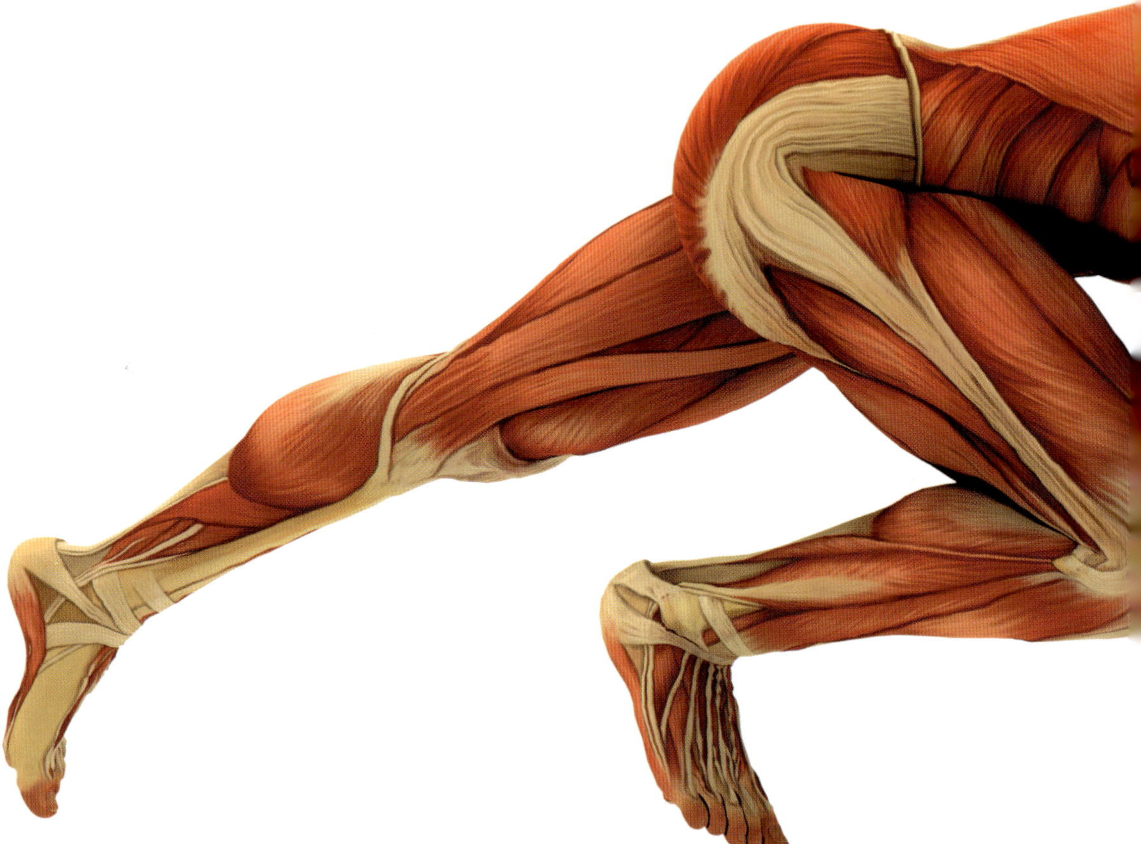

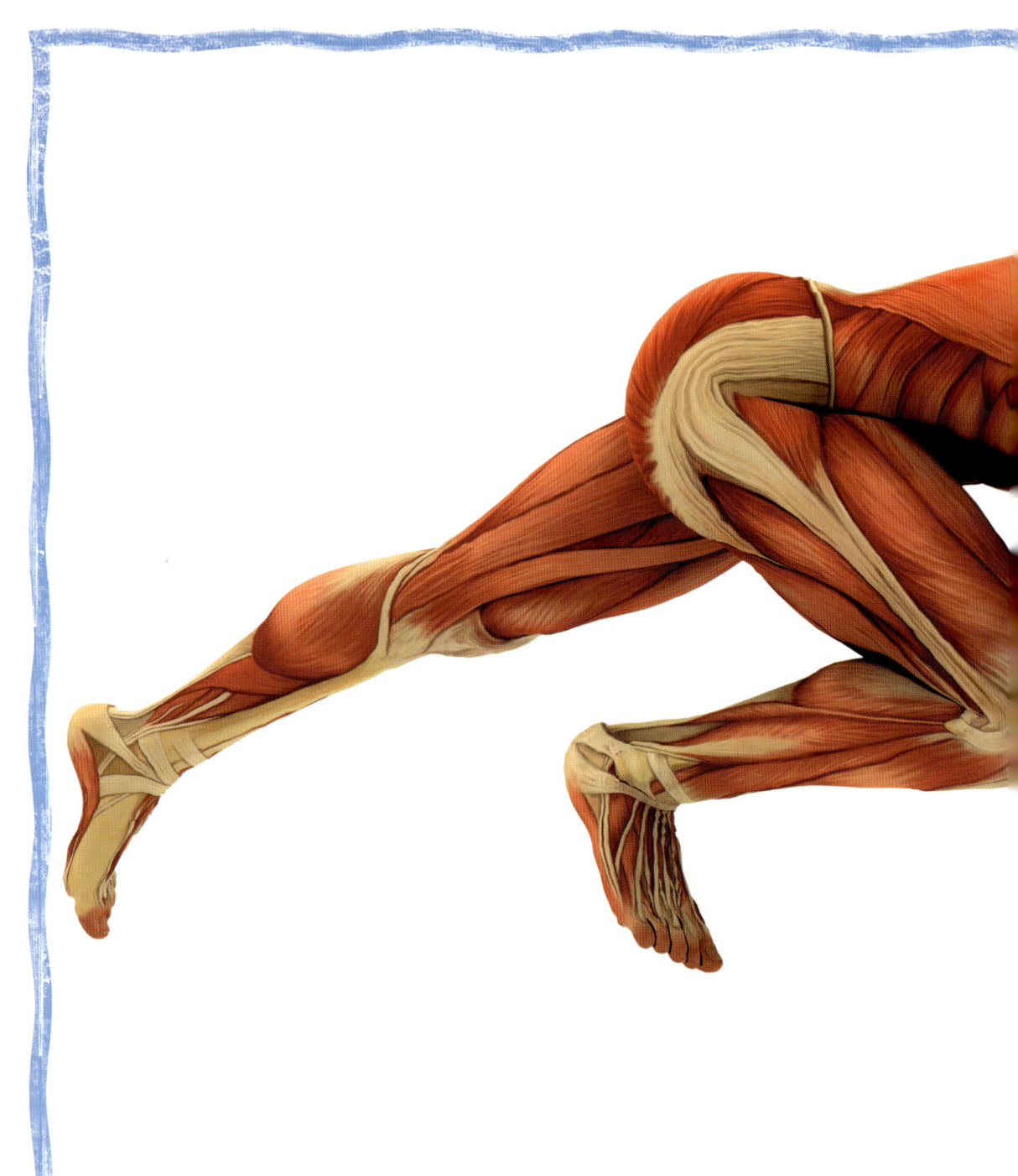

Human Body

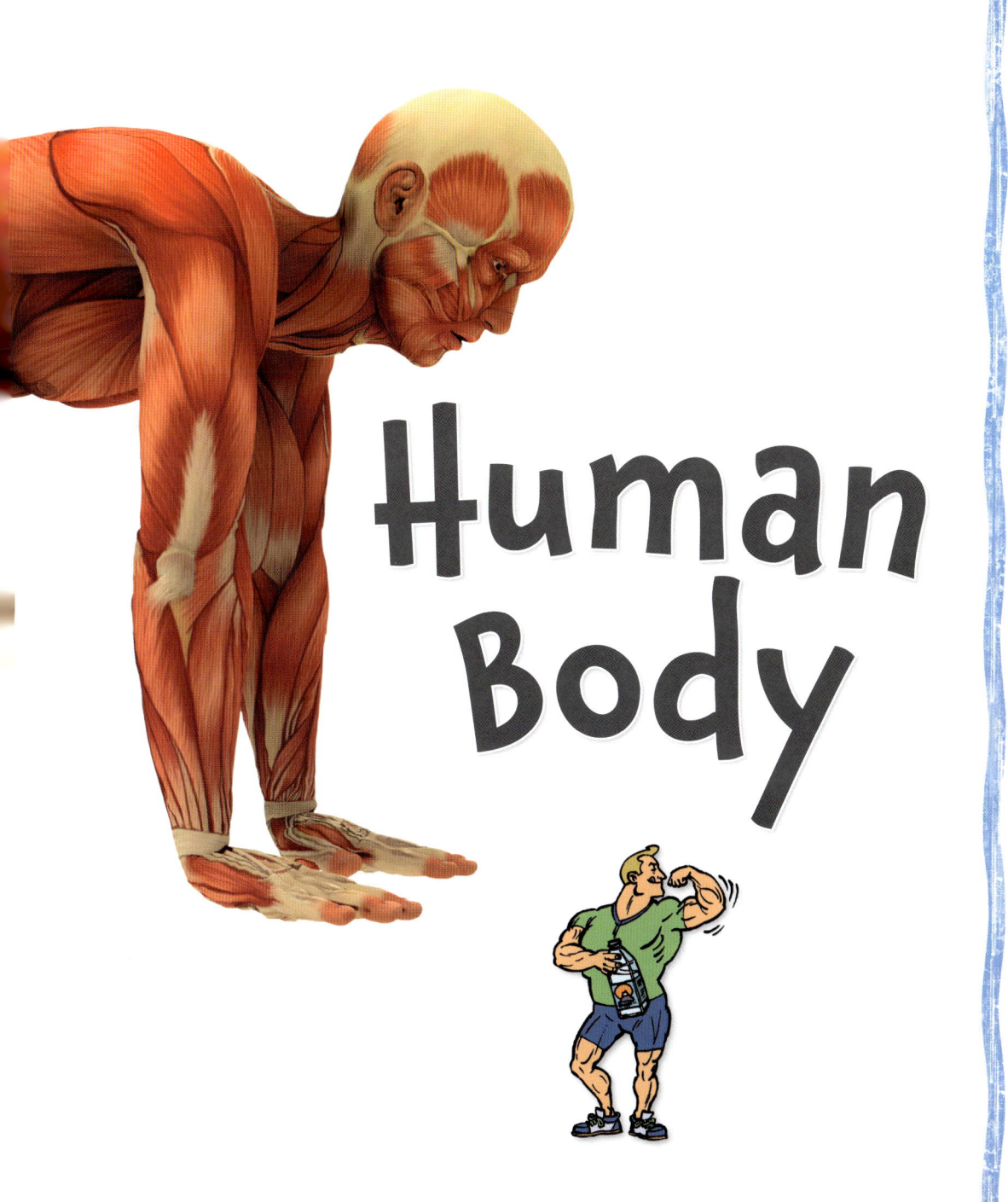

why do babies grip so tightly?

Tiny babies can do simple things. If something touches a baby's cheek, it turns its head and tries to suck. If something touches the baby's hand, it grips tightly. These actions are called reflexes. They help the baby survive.

Giant baby

A baby grows quickly before it is born. If it grew this fast for 50 years, it would be taller than Mount Everest!

Baby gripping

When do babies start to walk?

Usually when they are about one year old. Babies can roll over at three months. At six months, they can sit up. At nine months they start to crawl. Then babies learn to stand and take their first steps.

Find out
Why do you think a newborn baby cries? Ask a grown-up if you need any help.

Am I always learning?

Yes, you are! Most children start school when they are five years old. They learn to count, read, write and draw. Children learn outside of the classroom, too. Playing and having fun with friends is a great way to learn new things!

Children playing

what does my skin do?

Skin protects you from bumps and scratches. It stops your body from drying out, and prevents germs from getting in. When you play on bikes or skateboards, you should wear gloves and knee pads to protect your skin.

Gloves protect from scrapes

Knee pads protect from cuts

Ouch! Ouch! Ouch!

There are millions of tiny touch sensors in your skin. They tell your brain when something touches your skin. Some sensors feel hot and cold. Others feel pain. Ouch!

How thick is my skin?

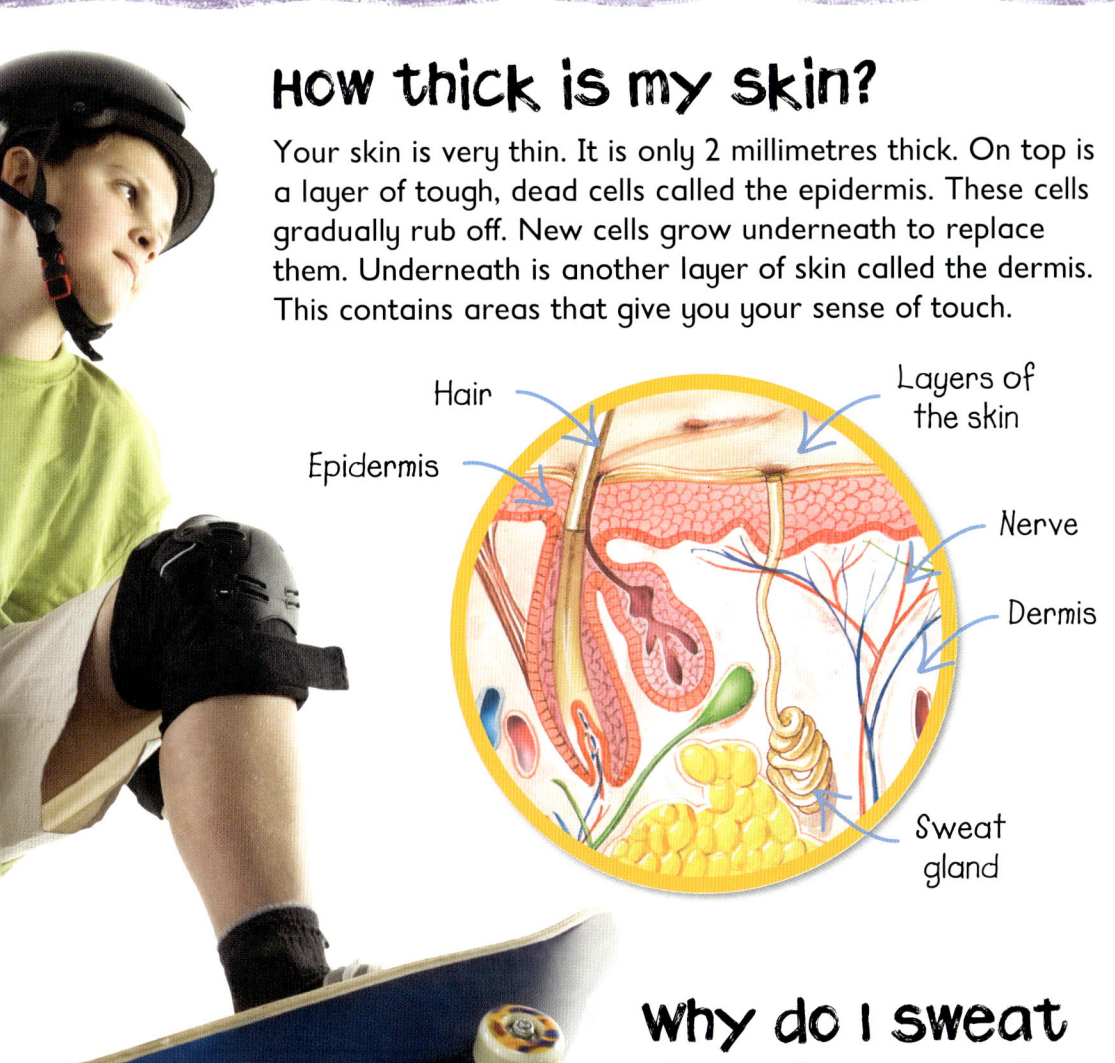

Your skin is very thin. It is only 2 millimetres thick. On top is a layer of tough, dead cells called the epidermis. These cells gradually rub off. New cells grow underneath to replace them. Underneath is another layer of skin called the dermis. This contains areas that give you your sense of touch.

Hair
Layers of the skin
Epidermis
Nerve
Dermis
Sweat gland

Why do I sweat when I'm warm?

To cool down again. Your body warms up on a hot day or when you run about. You sweat to get rid of the heat. Your body lets sweat out through your skin. As the sweat dries, it takes away heat. This cools you down.

Think
If you are riding a bike or playing on a skateboard, what should you wear on your head, and why?

How much hair do I have?

Your whole body is covered in about five million hairs! You have about 100,000 hairs on your head. Hair grows out of tiny pits in your skin, called follicles. It grows in different colours and can be wavy, curly or straight.

Blonde wavy hair

Brown straight hair

Red straight hair

Black curly hair

What are nails made from?

Fingernails and toenails are made from a hard material called keratin. This is the same material that hair is made from. Nails grow out of the nail root. In a week, a nail grows about half a millimetre. They grow faster at night than in the day!

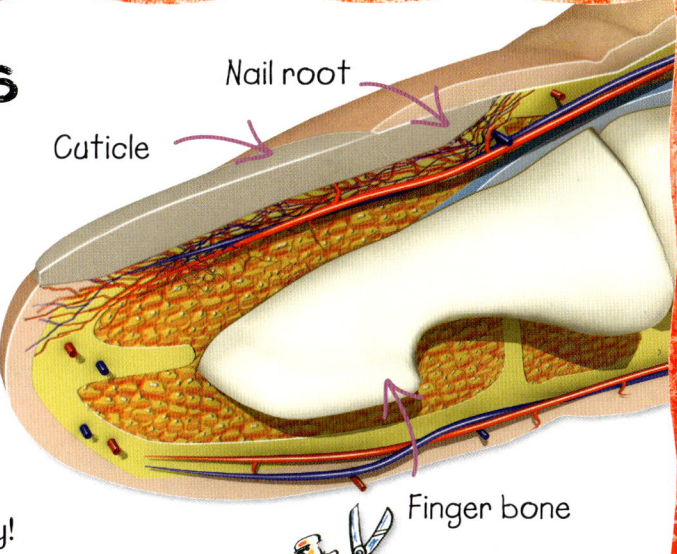

Nail root

Cuticle

Finger bone

Finger nail

For the chop
The hair on your head grows about 2 millimetres a week. If a hair is never cut, it reaches about one metre in length before falling out. It is replaced by a new hair.

Look
Have a look in the mirror. Is your hair straight, wavy or curly? Use the picture on page 40 to help you.

Why do we have fingernails?

Fingernails protect your fingertips. The nail stops your fingertip bending back when you touch something. This helps your fingers to feel things. Nails are useful for picking up tiny objects.

How many bones do I have?

Most people have 206 bones. Half of them are in your hands and feet. All your bones together make up your skeleton. The skeleton is like a frame. It holds up the other parts of your body. It also protects the squashy bits inside.

Human skeleton →

Find
Can you find your collarbone? It starts at your shoulder and runs to the top of your rib cage.

Skeleton key
① Skull
② Collar bone
③ Shoulder blade
④ Ribs
⑤ Upper arm bone
⑥ Pelvis
⑦ Thigh bone
⑧ Kneecap
⑨ Calf bone
⑩ Shin bone

strong bones

Your bone is lightweight but super-strong. It is stronger than concrete or steel, which are used for making buildings and bridges! But bones can still break if they are bent too much.

what are bones made from?

Bones are made from different materials mixed together. Some of the materials are very hard and some are tough and bendy. Together they make bones very strong. There is a kind of jelly called marrow inside some bones. This makes tiny parts for your blood, called red and white cells.

Marrow

Spongy bone

Hard bone

How are bones joined together?

Your bones are connected by joints. They let your back, arms, legs, fingers and toes move. You have about 100 joints in your body. The largest of your joints are in your hips and knees. The smallest joints are inside your ear.

How do muscles work?

Muscles are made from fibres that look like bits of string. The fibres get shorter to make the muscle pull. The biggest muscles in your body are in your bottom! You use them when you walk and run. The strongest muscle in your body is in your jaw.

Muscle

Muscle fibre

Nerve branches

How do joints bend?

Muscles make your joints, such as your elbows and knees, bend. They help you to run, jump, hold and lift things. In fact you need muscles to move all of your body.

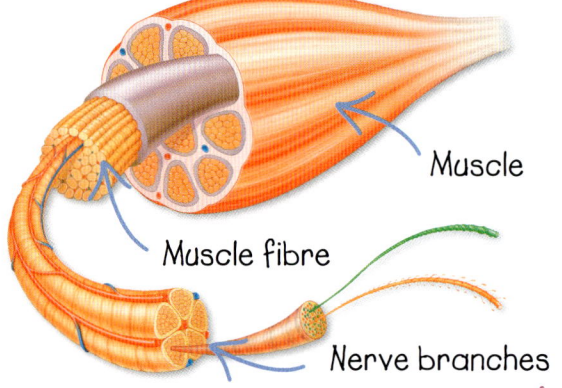

cheeky muscles

Your face is full of muscles. You use them to smile, to wrinkle your nose, or to cry. You use more muscles to frown than to smile!

What makes my muscles move?

Your brain does. It sends messages along nerves to your muscles. Lots of muscles are needed, even for small movements, like writing with a pen. Your brain controls other muscles without you thinking about it. For example, the muscles in your heart keep working even when you are asleep.

Human muscular skeleton

Feel
Bend and unbend your arm. Can you feel your arm muscles getting shorter and longer?

why do I need to breathe?

You breathe to take air into your body. There is a gas in the air called oxygen that your body needs to work. The air goes up your nose or into your mouth. Then it goes down a tube called the windpipe and into your lungs.

① Air goes into your nose or mouth

② Air goes down the windpipe

③ Air enters the lungs

count
How many times do you breathe in and out in one minute?

Is my voice kept in a box?

Not quite! The real name for your voicebox is the larynx. It's at the top of the windpipe, and makes a bulge at the front of your neck. Air passing through the voicebox makes it shake, or vibrate. This is the sound of your voice. Your voice can make lots of sounds, and helps you to sing!

Children singing

Fill 'em up

When you are resting, you take in enough air to fill a can of fizzy drink in every breath. When you are running, you breathe in ten times as much air.

What makes air go into my lungs?

There is a big muscle under your lungs that moves down. More muscles make your ribs move out, making your lungs bigger. Air rushes into your lungs to fill the space and when your muscles relax, the air is pushed out again.

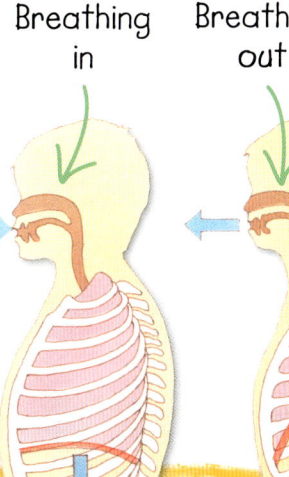

Breathing in

Breathing out

What food is good for me?

Bread gives energy

Lots of food is good for you! Different foods give your body the goodness it needs. Fruit and vegetables are very good for you. Bread and pasta give you energy. Small amounts of fat, such as cheese, keep your nerves healthy. Chicken and fish keep your muscles strong.

Fruit is full of goodness

Vegetables help digestion

Eating elephants

You eat about one kilogram of food every day. During your life, you will eat about 30 tonnes of food. That's the same weight as six elephants!

Draw
Look at the pictures on these pages. Can you draw a healthy meal that you would like to eat?

What happens when I swallow?

The first thing you do with food is chew it, then you swallow lumps of the chewed food. As you do this, the food goes down a tube called the oesophagus (gullet). Muscles in the oesophagus push the food into your stomach.

Fats keep nerves healthy

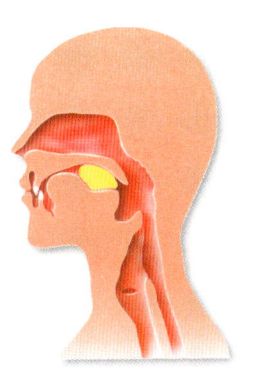

① Tongue pushes food to the back of the throat

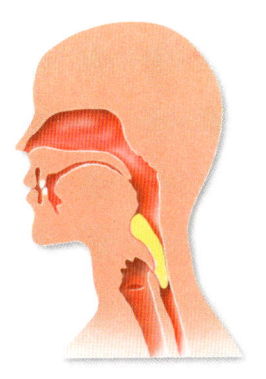

② Throat muscles squeeze the food downwards

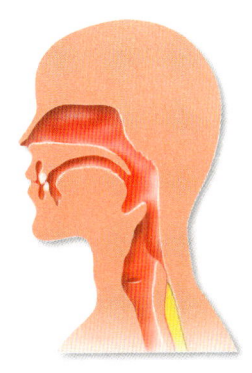

③ The oesophagus pushes food to the stomach

Fish helps muscles to grow strong

Sugars are needed in small quantities

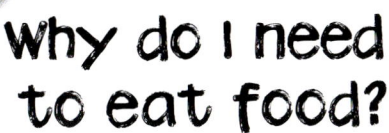

Why do I need to eat food?

Food keeps your body working. It is like fuel for your body. It keeps your body going through the day and night, and works your muscles. Food also contains things your body needs to grow, repair itself and fight illness.

49

What are teeth made of?

Teeth are covered in a material called enamel. This is harder than most kinds of rock! Teeth are fixed into your jaw bones by roots. Sharp front teeth (incisors) bite food into small pieces. Tall, pointy teeth (canines) tear and pull food. Flat back teeth (molars) chew food to a mush.

Canine

Incisor

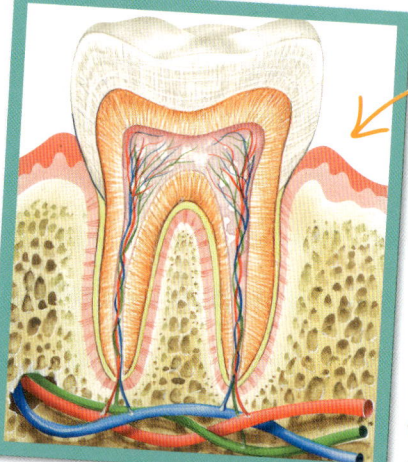

Molar

Root

Inside a tooth

How many sets of teeth do I have?

You have two sets. A baby is born without teeth. The first set of teeth appears when a child is six months old. This set has 20 teeth. These teeth usually start to fall out at about seven years old, and are replaced by 32 adult teeth.

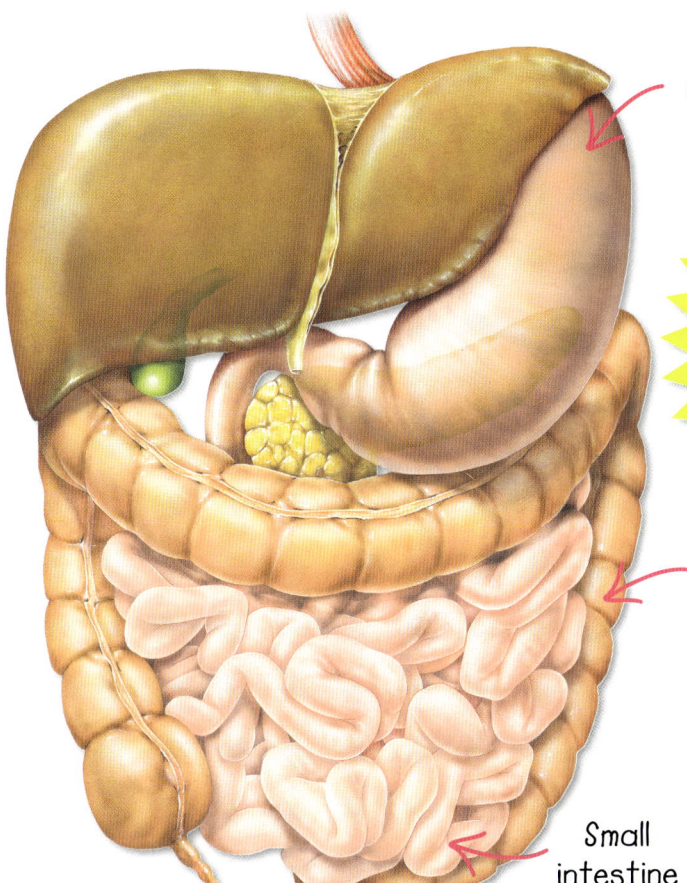

Stomach

Large intestine

Small intestine

Rectum

Discover
Do you still have your first set of teeth, or have your baby teeth begun to fall out?

What happens to the food I swallow?

The food you swallow goes into your stomach. Here, special juices and strong muscles break the food up into a thick mush. The mushy food then goes into a long tube called the intestines. Here, all the goodness from the food is taken out, to be used by our body.

All gone
When you go to the toilet, you get rid of waste. This is leftover food. It is stored in your large intestine until you go to the toilet.

51

Why does my heart beat?

Blood from body

Blood to lungs

Blood from lung

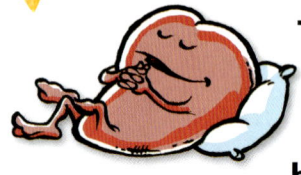

To pump blood and oxygen around your body. Your heart is about the size of your fist and is made of muscle. When it beats, your heart squeezes blood into tubes. These tubes carry blood and oxygen around your body. The blood then comes back to the heart from the lungs, with more oxygen.

Blood from body

Beat of life
Your heart beats once a second for the whole of your life. That is 86,000 beats a day, and 31 million beats a year. In total, this is 2000 million beats in your life.

what does blood do?

Your whole body needs oxygen to work. Blood carries oxygen to every part of your body in its red cells. Blood also contains white cells that fight germs. Tubes called arteries and veins carry blood around your body.

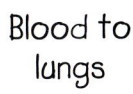

Blood to body

Blood to lungs

Blood from lung

Blood to body

Feel
Touch your neck under your chin. Can you feel the blood flowing through an artery to your brain?

Does blood get dirty?

Yes, it does. Because blood carries waste away from your body parts, it has to be cleaned. This is done by your kidneys. They take the waste out of the blood and make a liquid called urine. This liquid leaves your body when you go to the toilet.

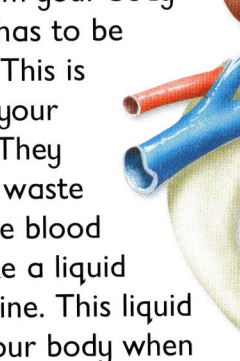

Kidney

Are my eyes like a camera?

Your eyes work like a tiny camera. They collect light that bounces off the things you are looking at. This makes tiny pictures at the back of the eyes. Here, millions of sensors pick up the light. They send a picture to your brain along a nerve.

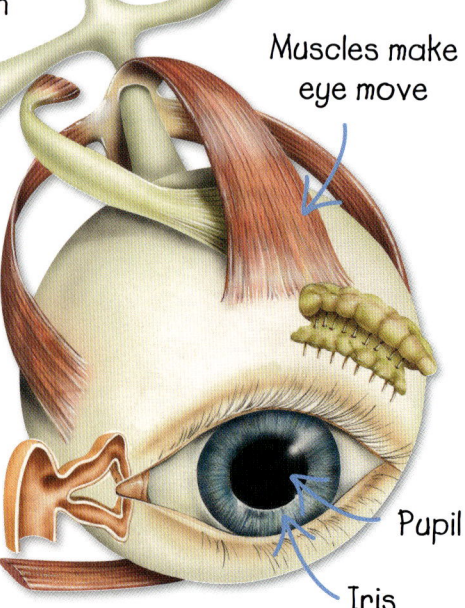

LOOK
Look in the mirror at your eye. Can you see the dark pupil where light goes in?

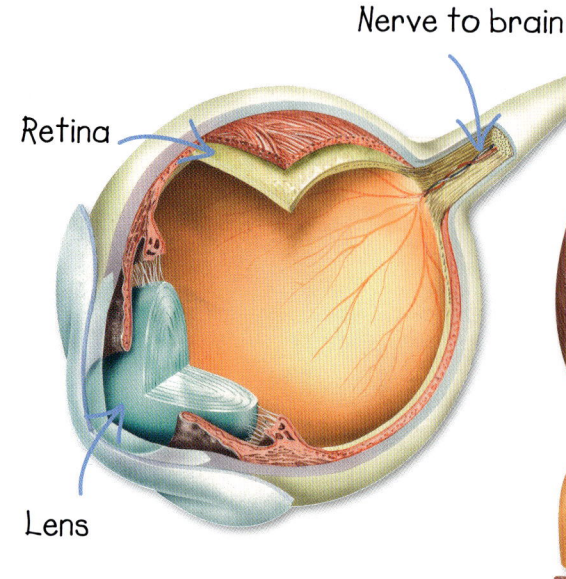

- Nerve to brain
- Muscles make eye move
- Retina
- Lens
- Pupil
- Iris

Ear bones

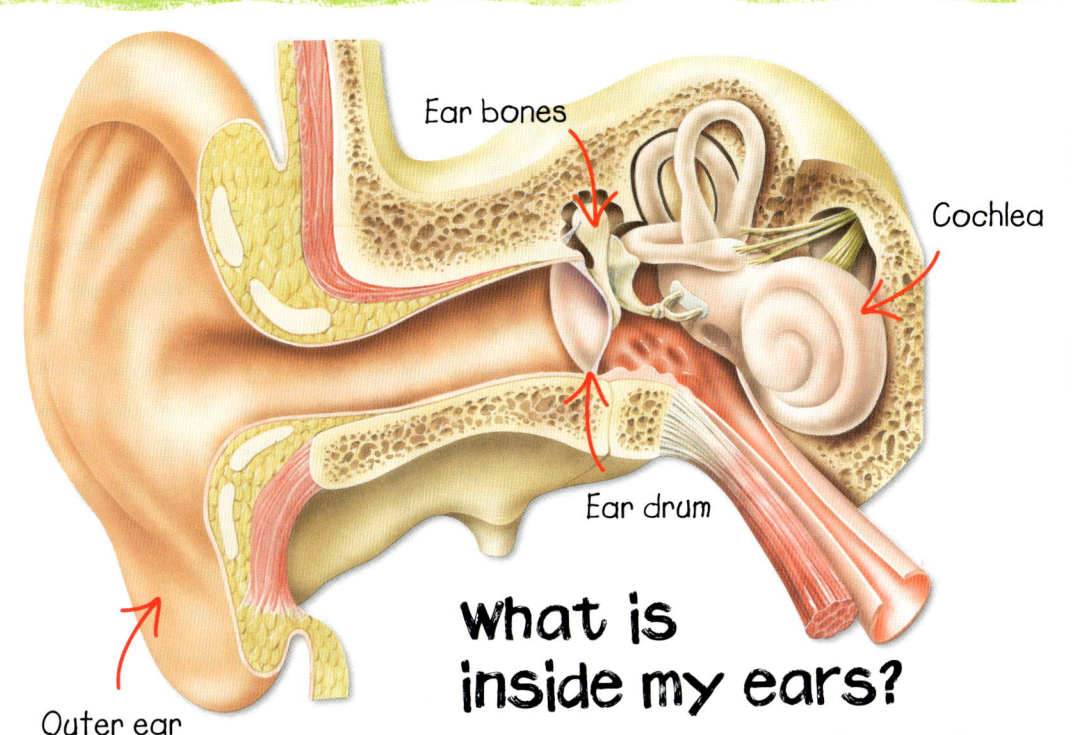

Cochlea

Ear drum

Outer ear

What is inside my ears?

The flap on your head is only part of your ear. The hole in your ear goes to a tiny piece of tight skin, called an eardrum. Sounds enter your ear and make the eardrum move in and out. Tiny bones pass these movements to the cochlea, which is shaped like a snail. This is filled with liquid.

How do I hear sounds?

The cochlea in your ear contains thousands of tiny hairs. It is also full of liquid. Sounds make the liquid move. This makes the hairs wave about. Tiny sensors pick up the waving, and send messages to your brain so you hear the sound.

In a spin

Inside your ear are loops full of liquid. They can tell if you move your head. This helps you to balance. If you spin around, the fluid keeps moving. This makes you feel dizzy!

Why can't I see smells?

Smell sensors

Because they're invisible! Smells are tiny particles that float in the air. Inside the top of your nose are sticky smell sensors. When you sniff something, the sensors collect the smell particles. They send messages to your brain, which tell you what you can smell.

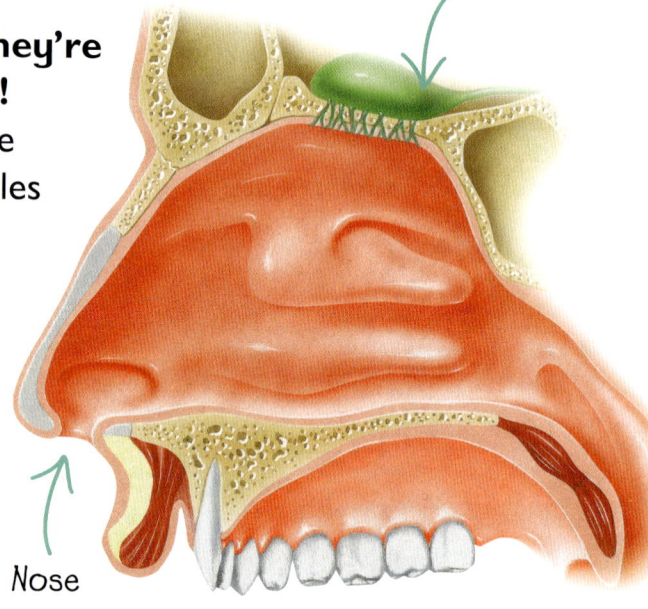

Nose

A blocked dose!

Smell and taste work together when you eat. Your sense of smell helps you to taste flavours in food. When you have a cold, your smell sensors get blocked, so you cannot taste, either.

How many smells can I sense?

Your nose can sense about 3000 different smells. You don't just have a sense of smell so you can smell nice things, such as flowers and perfumes! Your sense of smell warns you if food is rotten before you eat it.

Think
Can you think of three different things that taste sour, sweet and salty?

How do I taste things?

With your tongue. Your tongue is covered with tiny taste buds. The buds sense flavours and send a signal to your brain, which tells you if something is sweet or savoury. Your tongue also moves food around your mouth and helps you to speak.

Taste bud

Tongue

Muscle of tongue

Is my brain really big?

Your brain is about the same size as your two fists put together. It is the place where you think, remember, feel happy or sad – and dream. Your brain also takes information from your senses and controls your body. The main part is called the cerebrum.

Cerebrum

Cerebellum controls muscles

Brain stem

Right and left
The main part of your brain is divided into two halves. The right half helps you to play music and to draw. The left half is good at thinking.

Can my brain really wave?

Brain waves from an EEG machine

Well, sort of! Your brain works using electricity. It has about 10,000 million tiny nerve cells. Tiny bursts of electricity are always jumping around between the cells. Doctors can see your brain working by looking at the electricity with a special machine called an EEG. It shows the electricity as waves on a screen.

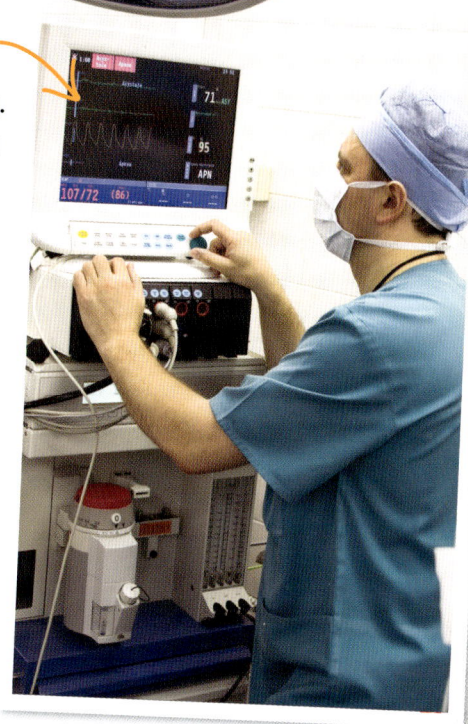

Find out
Your brain controls your five senses. Can you find out what they are?

How does my brain help me to play?

Different parts of your brain do different jobs. One part senses touch. Another part deals with thinking. Speaking is controlled by a different part. The cerebellum controls all your muscles. When you play and run, the cerebellum sends messages to your muscles to make them move.

How can I stay healthy?

There are things you can do to stop getting ill. The easiest thing is to eat the right food your body needs, such as fruit and vegetables. Try not to eat too much salty or sugary food. Exercise, such as riding a bike will keep your bones, muscles and heart healthy.

Getting old

Your body changes as you get old. You get shorter, your skin wrinkles and your hair might go grey. But if you stay fit and healthy you could live to be 100!

What can make me sick?

Lots of things can make you sick. Illnesses such as tummy upsets are caused by germs that get into your body. You can help to stop catching germs by washing your hands before eating and after going to the toilet.

Washing your hands with hot soapy water kills germs

Why do I have injections?

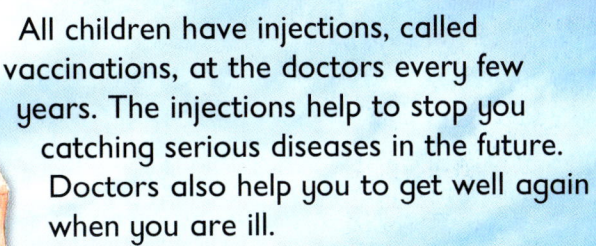

All children have injections, called vaccinations, at the doctors every few years. The injections help to stop you catching serious diseases in the future. Doctors also help you to get well again when you are ill.

Riding a bike can keep you healthy

Vaccinations protect us

Read

What should you do before meal times and after going to the toilet? Read this page again to find out.

Quiz time

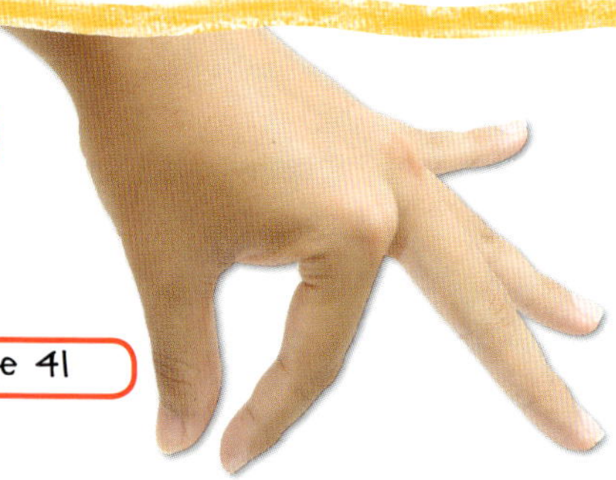

Do you remember what you have read about your body? These questions will test your memory. The pictures will help you. If you get stuck, read the pages again.

page 41

3. Why do we have fingernails?

page 43

4. How are bones joined together?

5. How do muscles work?

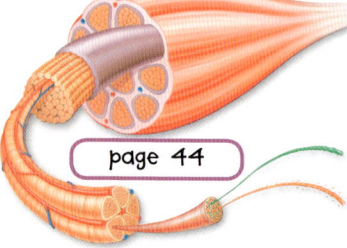

page 44

page 37

1. Am I always learning?

6. What makes air go into my lungs?

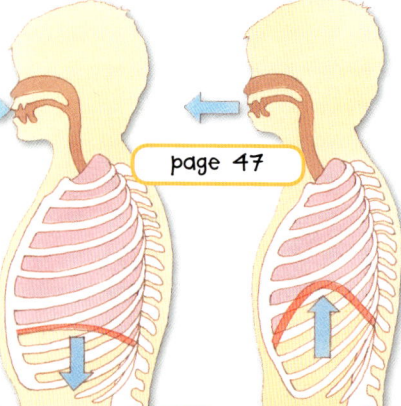

2. Why do I sweat when I'm warm?

page 47

page 39

62

7. Why do I need to eat food?

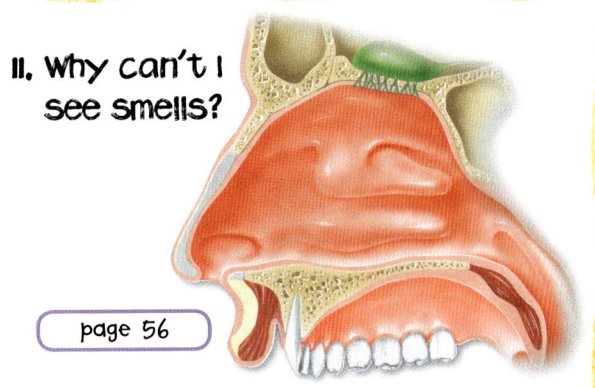

page 49

8. How many sets of teeth do I have?

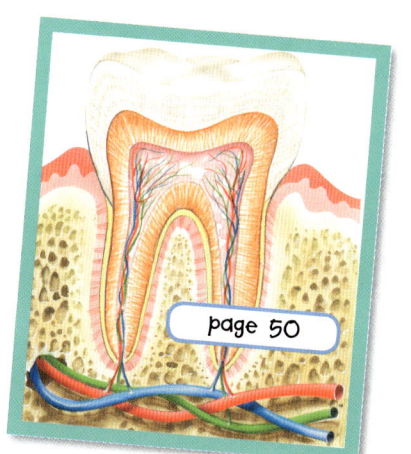

page 50

9. What does blood do?

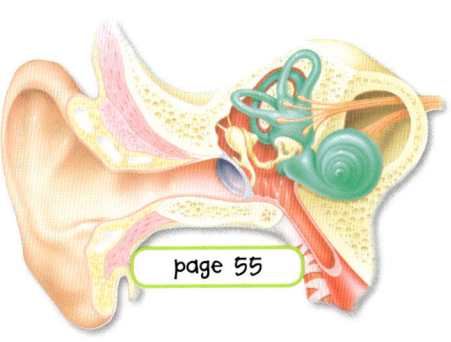

page 53

10. How do I hear sounds?

page 55

11. Why can't I see smells?

page 56

12. How does my brain help me to play?

page 59

13. What can make me sick?

page 61

Answers

1. Yes, you are
2. To help you cool down again
3. To protect our fingertips
4. They are connected by joints
5. The fibres inside get shorter and pull
6. Muscles
7. To keep your body working
8. Two sets
9. Carries oxygen around your body
10. With the parts that are inside your ear
11. Smells are tiny particles
12. It tells your muscles to move
13. Germs

63

64

Planet Earth

where did the Earth come from?

A cloud of dust spun around the Sun

The Earth came from a cloud of dust. The dust whizzed around the Sun at speed and began to stick together to form lumps of rock. The rocks crashed into each other to make planets, and one of them was the Earth.

why does the Moon look lumpy?

Big rocks from space, called meteorites, have crashed into the Moon and made dents on its surface. These dents are called craters and they give the Moon a lumpy appearance.

Lumps of rock began to form

LOOK
At night, use some binoculars to look at the Moon. Can you see craters on its surface?

The Earth was formed from the lumps of rock

What is the Earth made of?

The Earth is a huge ball-shaped lump of rock. Most of the Earth's surface is covered by water – this makes the seas and oceans. Rock that is not covered by water makes the land.

Face the Moon
The Moon travels around the Earth. As the Moon doesn't spin, we only ever see one side of its surface.

Why does the Earth spin?

The Earth is always spinning. This is because it was made from a spinning cloud of gas and dust. As it spins, the Earth leans a little to one side. It takes the Earth 24 hours to spin around once. This period of time is called a day.

Morning

Evening

Spinning Earth

Discover

There are 24 hours in a day. How many minutes are there in one hour?

Hot and cold

In the Caribbean, the sea can be as warm as a bath. In the Arctic, it is so cold, that often the sea freezes over.

Mid-day

The Sun

Why do we have day and night?

Every day, each part of the Earth spins towards the Sun, and then away from it. When a part of the Earth is facing the Sun, it is daytime there. When that part is facing away from Earth, it is night time.

Night

Do people live on the Moon?

No, they don't. There is no air on the Moon so people cannot live there. Astronauts have visited the Moon in space rockets. They wear special equipment to help them breathe.

69

What is inside the Earth?

Crust

There are different layers inside the Earth. There is a thin, rocky crust, a solid area called the mantle and a centre called the core. The outer part of the core is made of hot, liquid metal. The inner core is made of solid metal.

Natural magnet

Near the centre of the Earth is hot, liquid iron. As the Earth spins, the iron behaves like a magnet. This is why a compass needle points to North and South.

Find
Use a compass to find North. Does the needle move when you do?

Active volcano

Mantle

Inner core

Outer core

Can we travel into the Earth?

No, we can't. The Earth's core is incredibly hot and so far down that no one could ever go there. Sometimes, boiling-hot liquid rock bursts up through the Earth's surface from mountains called volcanoes.

Mountains

Does the ground move?

The Earth's crust is split into huge areas called plates. Each plate is moving very slowly. If the plates move apart from each other they may cause earthquakes. If they move towards each other they may form volcanoes or mountains.

what is a fossil?

Scientists digging up and studying fossils

A fossil was once a living thing that has now turned to stone. By studying fossils, scientists can learn more about the past and how animals, such as dinosaurs, used to live.

A trilobite was an ancient sea creature

How is a fossil made?

It takes millions of years to make a fossil. When an animal dies, it may be buried by sand. The soft parts of its body rot away, leaving just bones, teeth or shells. These slowly turn to rock and a fossil forms.

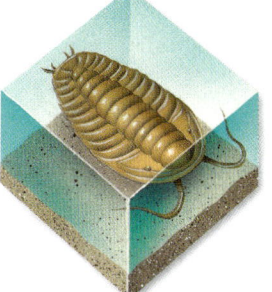

Explore
Look for rocks in your garden. They may be so old, dinosaurs could have trodden on them.

① The trilobite dies

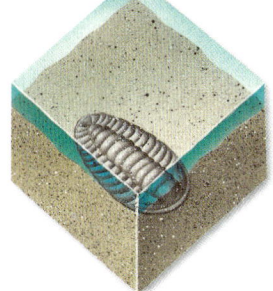

② The trilobite gets covered with mud

③ The mud turns to stone

④ The fossil forms inside the stone

Cave houses
In Turkey, some people live in rocky caves. These huge cone-shaped rocks stay very cool in the hot weather.

Rock fall

Why do rocks crumble?

When a rock is warmed up by the Sun it gets a little bigger. When it cools down, the rock shrinks to its original size. If this process happens to a rock too often, it starts to crumble away.

What is a volcano?

Erupting volcano

Liquid rock

A volcano is a mountain that sometimes shoots hot, liquid rock out of its top. Deep inside a volcano is an area called the magma chamber. This is filled with liquid rock. If pressure builds up in the chamber, the volcano may explode, and liquid rock will shoot out of the top.

Magma chamber

Colour
Draw a picture of a volcano erupting. Remember to colour the lava bright red.

What is a range?
A range is the name for a group of mountains. The biggest ranges are the Alps in Europe, the Andes in South America, the Rockies in North America and the highest of all – the Himalayas in Asia.

How are mountains made?
One way that mountains are formed is when the Earth's plates crash together. The crust at the edge of the plates slowly crumples and folds. Over millions of years this pushes up mountains. The Himalayan Mountains in Asia were made this way.

Mountain range is pushed up

Layer on layer
When a volcano erupts, the hot lava cools and forms a rocky layer. With each new eruption, another layer is added and the volcano gets bigger.

Why are there earthquakes?

Earthquakes happen when the plates in the Earth's crust move apart suddenly, or rub together. They start deep underground in an area called the focus. Land above the focus is shaken violently. The worst part of the earthquake happens above the focus, in an area called the epicentre.

Epicentre

Focus

Remember
Can you remember what it is that breaks at level 5 on the Richter Scale?

What is the Richter Scale?

The Richter Scale measures the strength of an earthquake. It starts at level 1 and goes up to level 8. The higher the number, the more powerful and destructive the earthquake.

Super senses

Some people believe that animals can sense when an earthquake is about to happen!

Windows break at level 5

Bridges and buildings collapse at level 7

Widespread destruction at level 8

Can earthquakes start fires?

Yes, a powerful earthquake can cause fires. In 1906, a huge earthquake in San Francisco, USA caused lots of fires. The fires burnt down most of the city and the people who lived there became homeless.

What is a glacier?

Moving glacier

Glaciers are huge rivers of ice found near the tops of mountains. Snow falls on the mountain and becomes squashed to make ice. The ice forms a glacier that slowly moves down the mountainside until it melts.

Fancy flakes

Snowflakes are made of millions of tiny ice crystals. No two snowflakes are the same, as the ice crystals make millions of different shapes.

Melted ice

can ice be fun?

Yes, it can! Many people go ice skating and they wear special boots with blades on them called ice skates. Figure skaters are skilled athletes who compete to win prizes.

LOOK
Next time it snows, put some gloves on and let the snowflakes fall into your hand. Can you see crystals?

Iceberg

what is an iceberg?

Icebergs are big chunks of ice that have broken off glaciers and drifted into the sea. Only a small part of the iceberg can be seen above the water. The main part of the iceberg is hidden under the water.

Where do rivers flow to?

Rivers flow to the sea or into lakes. They start off as small streams in hills and mountains. The streams flow downhill, getting bigger and wider. The place where a river meets the sea, or flows into a lake, is called the river mouth.

River mouth

Discover
Try to find out the name of the highest waterfall in the world. Where is it?

Waterfall

Why are there waterfalls?

Waterfalls are made when water wears down rocks to make a cliff face. The water then falls over the edge into a deep pool called a plunge pool. Waterfalls may only be a few centimetres high, or several hundred metres high!

A river begins in the mountains

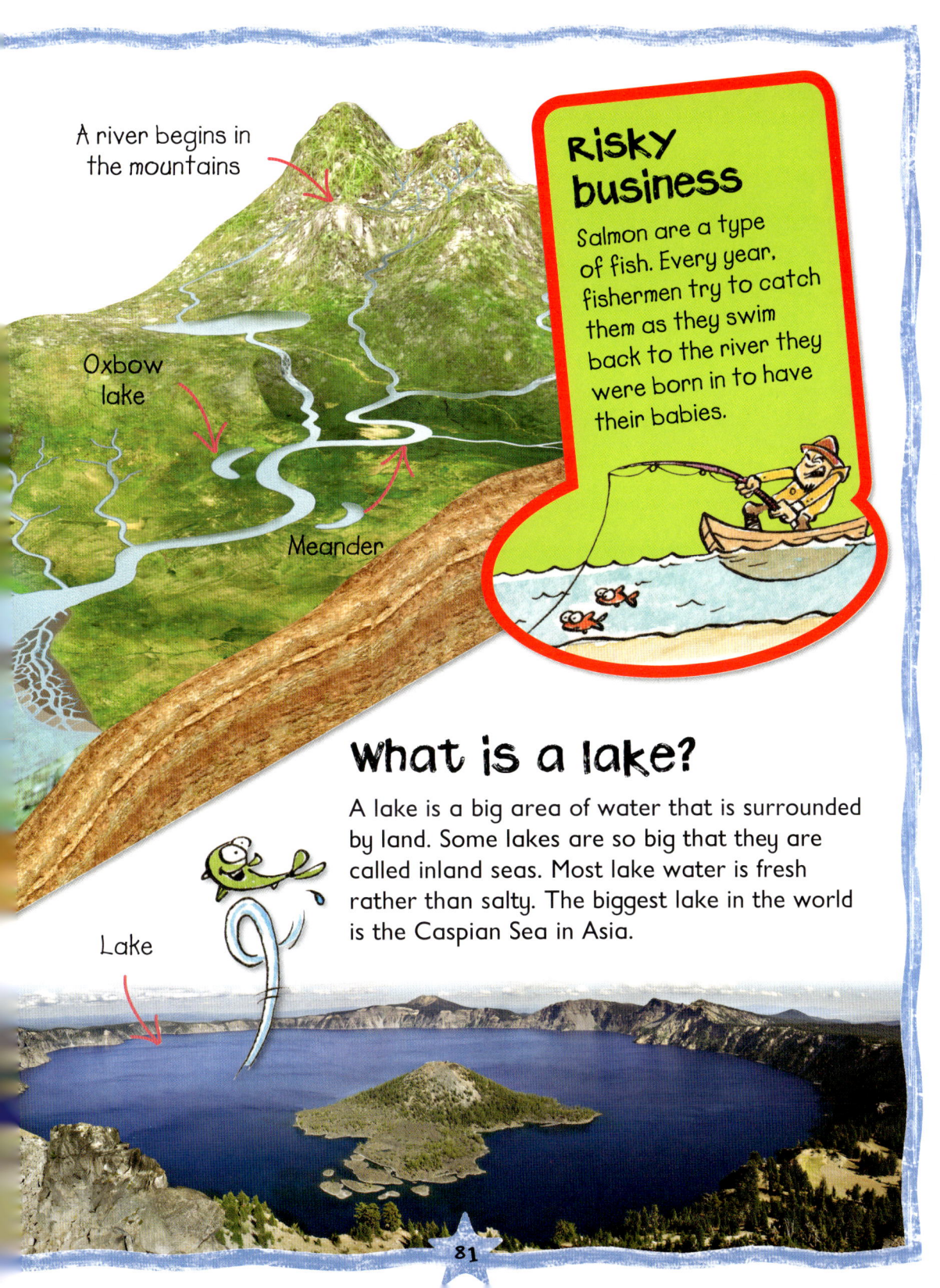

Oxbow lake

Meander

Risky business

Salmon are a type of fish. Every year, fishermen try to catch them as they swim back to the river they were born in to have their babies.

What is a lake?

A lake is a big area of water that is surrounded by land. Some lakes are so big that they are called inland seas. Most lake water is fresh rather than salty. The biggest lake in the world is the Caspian Sea in Asia.

Lake

Are there volcanoes under the sea?

Yes, there are. Volcanoes and mountains lie hidden in deep oceans. The ocean floor is flat and is called a plain. Mountains and volcanoes may rise across the plain, and some break the ocean's surface to form new islands.

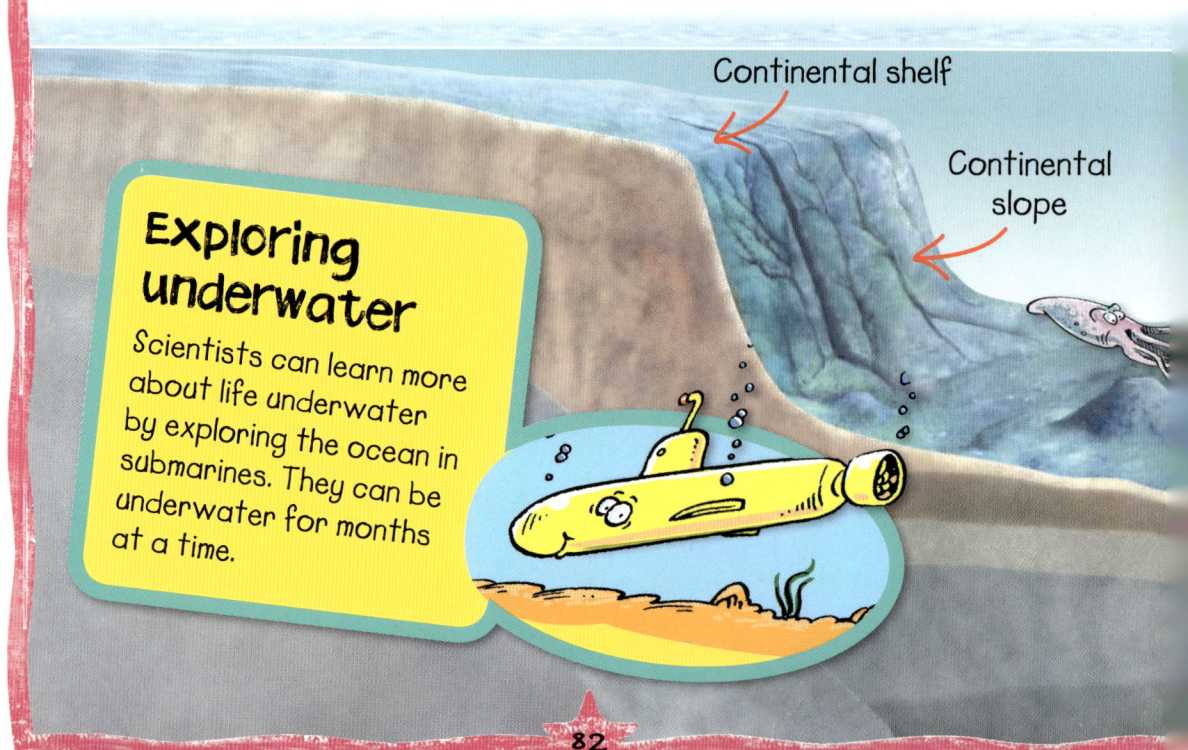

Continental shelf

Continental slope

Exploring underwater

Scientists can learn more about life underwater by exploring the ocean in submarines. They can be underwater for months at a time.

Why do coasts change?

The coast is where the land meets the sea, and it is always changing. In many places, waves crash onto land and rocks, slowly breaking them up. This can change the shape of the coastline.

Coastline

Coral reef

What is coral?

Coral is made from polyps. These are tiny creatures the size of pin heads that live in warm, shallow waters. The polyps join together in large groups and create rocky homes. These are called coral reefs.

Underwater volcano

Find out

Have a look in an atlas to find out which ocean you live closest to.

Plain   Ridge   Trench

How are caves made?

When rain falls on rock, it can make caves. Rainwater mixes with a gas in the air called carbon dioxide. This makes a strong acid. The acid can attack the rock and make it disappear. Underground, the rainwater makes caves in which streams and lakes can be found.

Underground cave

Can lava make caves?

When a volcano erupts and lava flows through the mountain, it can carve out a cave. A long time after the eruption, when the volcano is no longer active, people can walk through this lava cave without having to bend down.

Lava cave

Stalactites

Super spiky
Stalagmites grow up from the cave floor. Dripping water leaves a rocky substance that grows into a rocky spike.

What is a stalactite?

Rocky spikes that hang from cave ceilings are called stalactites. When water drips from the cave ceiling, it leaves tiny amounts of a rocky substance behind. Very slowly, over a long period of time, this grows into a stalactite.

Remember
Stalactites hold on tight, stalagmites might reach the top!

Stalagmites

Is there water in the desert?

Yes, there is. Deserts sometimes get rain. This rainwater seeps into the sand and collects in rock. The water then builds up and forms a pool called an oasis. Plants grow around the oasis and animals visit the pool to drink.

what are grasslands?

Grasslands are found when there is too much rain for a desert but not enough rain for a forest. Large numbers of animals can be found living and feeding on grasslands, including zebras, antelopes and lions.

What is a rainforest?

In hot places, such as South America, there are areas of thick, green forest. These are rainforests, and they are home to amazing plants and animals. Rainforests have rainy weather all year round.

Draw
Create a picture of a camel crossing a desert. Don't forget to include its wide feet!

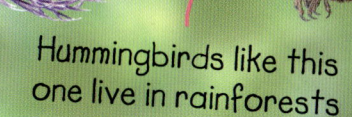

Hummingbirds like this one live in rainforests

Oasis

Big feet
Camels have wide feet that stop them sinking into the sand. They can also store water in their bodies for a long time.

where does rain come from?

Rain comes from the ocean! Water moves between the ocean, air and land in a water cycle. A fine mist of water rises into the air from the ocean and from plants. This fine mist then forms clouds. Water can fall from the clouds as rain.

Water vapour rising from the ocean

Water falling as rain

Water vapour rising from plants

Rain flows into rivers

Head in the clouds!

The tops of tall mountains are often in the clouds. At the top it looks misty. Mountaineers sometimes get lost in these clouds!

Cumulus

Stratus

Cirrus

Are all clouds small and fluffy?

Clouds come in lots of different shapes and sizes. Weather experts give the different clouds names. Fluffy clouds are called cumulus clouds. Some are small and some are giant. Flat clouds are called stratus clouds. Wispy clouds high in the sky are called cirrus clouds.

What rain never lands?

Sometimes rain that falls from a cloud never reaches the ground. If the drops of rain fall into very dry air, the water in them turns into gas. This means that the drops disappear and never reach the ground.

LOOK

Look at the clouds outside today. Are they fluffy or flat? The pictures above will help you.

What is snow made of?

Snow is made of ice, which is water that has frozen. When it is very cold in a cloud, tiny bits of ice (crystals) begin to form, instead of water drops. The pieces clump together to make snowflakes that fall to the ground. The weather must be very cold for snow to fall. If it is too warm, the snowflakes melt and turn to rain.

Shiver!
Antarctica is the coldest place on Earth. The lowest temperature ever recorded there is −89°C. That's much, much colder than inside a freezer!

Snow drifts

Avalanche

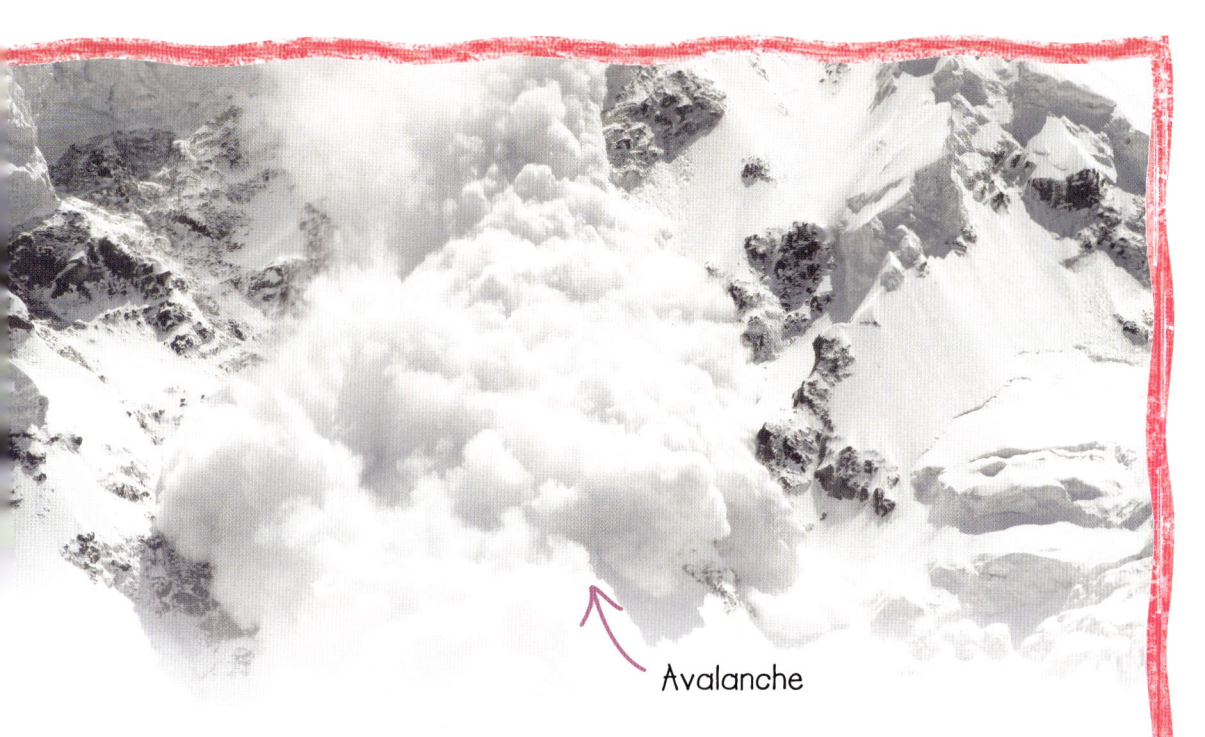

When is snow dangerous?

When lots of snow falls on mountains, deep layers build up on the slopes. The snow may suddenly slide down the mountain. This is an avalanche. A big avalanche can bury a town. A loud noise or even a person walking on the snow can start an avalanche.

Is snow really white?

Snow is actually made up of millions of individual snow crystals that are clear and colourless, not white. Each of these crystals has lots of tiny surfaces that reflect white light, so when you get big piles of them all together — as snow — it looks white.

Think
Can you think why it could be dangerous to ski across a steep hillside covered with snow?

where are the fastest winds?

Tornado

Inside a tornado. A tornado is like a spinning funnel made of air. They reach down from giant thunderstorms. The winds can blow at 480 kilometres an hour. That's twice as fast as an express train! Tornadoes can rip trees from the ground and destroy houses.

Which storm has an eye?

Eye

Hurricane hunter

A hurricane is a giant spinning storm made up of super-strong winds. The centre is a hole called the eye. Here it is calm and sunny. If a hurricane reaches land, the winds can damage buildings and heavy rain causes floods. Hurricane hunters are planes that fly into hurricanes to measure the wind speed.

Stormy names!

A tropical storm that starts in the Atlantic Ocean is called a hurricane. In the Pacific Ocean, a tropical storm is called a typhoon. In the Indian Ocean it is called a cyclone.

Draw

Look at the pictures on this page. Can you draw a picture of a tornado and a hurricane?

How do we measure wind?

We measure the wind on a scale called the Beaufort Scale. The slowest wind is Force 1 on the scale. This is called a light breeze. The strongest wind is Force 12. This is called a hurricane. Force zero means there is no wind at all.

What is a rainbow made of?

Rainbow

A rainbow is made of sunlight. The light bounces through raindrops. This splits the light into different colours. The colours of a rainbow are always the same. They are red, orange, yellow, green, blue, indigo and violet.

Northern lights

Remember
Can you remember all seven colours of a rainbow?

When does the sky have curtains?

In the far north and the far south of the world, amazing patterns of light sometimes appear in the sky. They look like colourful curtains. The patterns are called auroras (or-roar-rers). They happen when tiny light particles from the Sun smash into the air.

Rainbow with no colour!
A fogbow is a rainbow that is white. You might see a fogbow when the Sun shines through fog. It is white because the water drops in fog are too small to split up the light into rainbow colours.

When can you see three suns?

If there are thin clouds high in the sky, you might see three suns. The clouds are made of bits of ice. These bend light from the Sun. This makes it look as if there are two extra suns in the sky. We call these mock suns, or sun dogs.

Why is summer warm and sunny?

Spring in the north

The Earth is tipped to one side as it moves round the Sun. Some of the year, the north half of the Earth faces the Sun. Then the Sun is higher in the sky, making the weather warm. This is summer. When the southern half of the Earth faces the Sun, it is winter in the north.

Summer in the north

Sun

Why are days longer in summer?

Summer days are longer because the Earth is tilted and spins round. In summer, the Sun rises earlier and sets later. This makes daytime last longer than night. In the middle of summer in Sweden it is light for 21 hours!

Find
Can you find photographs of red, orange and brown leaves in autumn?

Winter in the north

Autumn colours

Why do leaves fall in autumn?

Autumn comes between summer and winter. Many trees lose their leaves in autumn because it is hard for them to grow in the dark winter months. The leaves turn from green to red, orange or brown. Then they fall to the ground.

Autumn in the north

Sunshine at midnight!
At the North and South Poles, the Sun never sets in summer. It is light all day. In winter, the Sun never rises. Then it is dark all day long!

How can we help the Earth?

Some of the things that people do can damage the Earth. Factories pump chemicals into the air and water. Forests are being cut down, killing the wildlife that lives there, and fumes from cars are clogging up the air. Scientists are trying to find new ways to protect the Earth before it is too late.

Help
Save all of your empty drinks cans and bottles and take them to your recycling centre.

Deforestation

Save the planet

There are lots of things we can do to protect our planet. Recycling, picking up litter, switching lights off and walking to the shops all help to make a difference.

How can we protect our planet?

Large areas of land have been made into national parks where wildlife is protected. People can go there to learn about both plants and animals.

Pond dipping

Wind turbines

What is renewable energy?

Burning coal and oil creates pollution, and in time these fuels will run out. Scientists are developing ways of using energy sources, such as wind, which replenish themselves naturally.

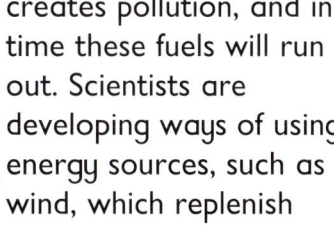

Quiz time

Do you remember what you have read about planet Earth? These questions will test your memory. The pictures will help you. If you get stuck, read the pages again.

3. What is inside the Earth?

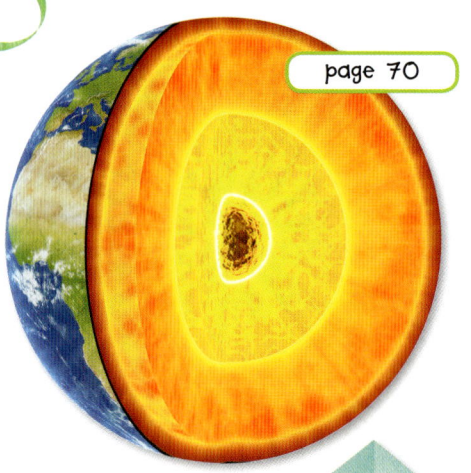

page 70

page 73

4. How is a fossil made?

5. What is a range?

page 75

page 66

1. Why does the Moon look lumpy?

6. What is the Richter scale?

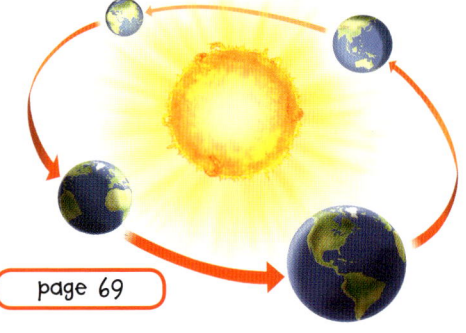

page 77

page 69

2. Why do we have day and night?

100

7. Can ice be fun?
page 79

8. What is an iceberg?
page 79

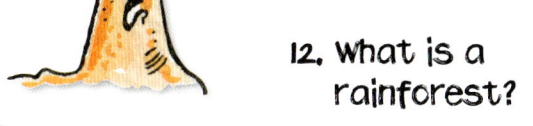

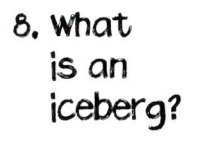

9. Why are there waterfalls?
page 80

10. Can lava make caves?
page 85

11. What is a stalactite?
page 85

12. What is a rainforest?
page 87

13. Which storm has an eye?
page 93

Answers
1. Because there are craters on its surface
2. Because the Earth is always spinning
3. Lots of different layers of rock and metal
4. By turning an animal's hard parts to rock over millions of years
5. A group of mountains
6. It measures the strength of an earthquake
7. Yes, people skate on ice for fun
8. A big chunk of ice that has broken off a glacier
9. Because water flows over cliffs
10. Yes it can
11. A rocky spike that hangs from the ceiling of a cave
12. A large, thick, green forest that grows in a hot place
13. The centre of a hurricane is called the eye

101

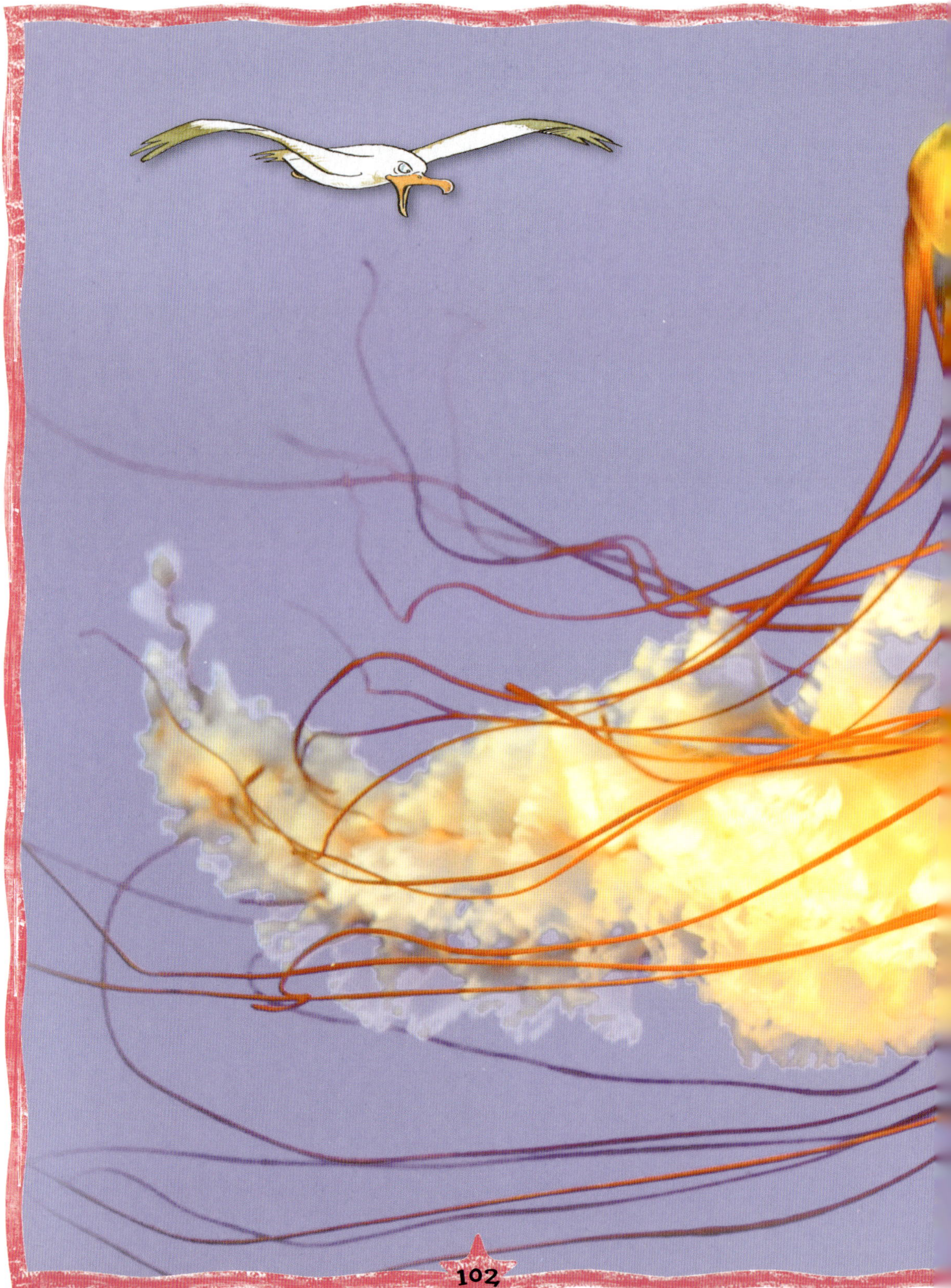

Oceans

Is there only one big ocean?

The Earth is covered by one giant ocean. We split this into five different oceans, which all flow into each other – the Arctic, Atlantic, Pacific, Indian and Southern. The land we live on, the continents, rises out of the oceans. More than two-thirds of the Earth's surface is covered by oceans – there is more than twice as much ocean as land!

Are there mountains under the sea?

Yes there are. The land beneath the sea looks a lot like the land above the sea. It is covered by mountains, flat areas called plains and deep valleys called trenches.

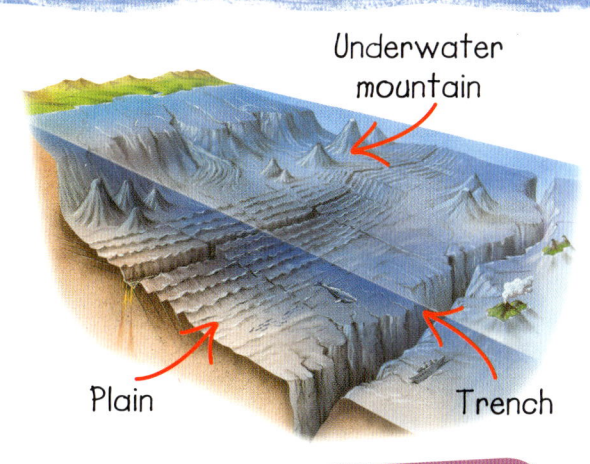

Underwater mountain

Plain

Trench

Salty and fresh

Almost all of the world's water is in the oceans. Only a tiny amount is in freshwater lakes and rivers.

Where do islands come from?

Islands are 'born' beneath the sea. If an underwater volcano erupts, it throws out hot, sticky lava. This cools and hardens in the water. Layers of lava build up and up, until a new island peeps above the waves.

Find
Look at the world map to find where you live. Which ocean is nearest to you?

Island

Do seashells have feet?

Tiny animals called limpets live inside some seashells. They stick to rocks at the shoreline where they eat slimy, green plants called algae. When the tide is out, limpets stick to the rocks like glue, with a strong muscular foot. They only move when the tide crashes in.

Limpets

Can starfish grow arms?

Yes they can. Starfish may have as many as 40 arms, called rays. If a hungry crab grabs hold of one, the starfish abandons its arm, and uses the others to get away. It then begins to grow a new arm.

Anemone

Starfish

Fighting fit

Anemones are a kind of sea-living plant. Some anemones fight over their feeding grounds. Beadlet anemones shoot sharp, tiny hooks at each other until the weakest one gives in.

When is a sponge like an animal?

Sponges are animals! They are simple creatures that filter food from sea water. They can be many different shapes, sizes and colours.

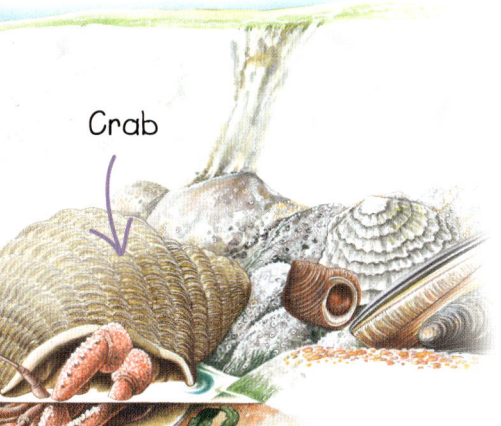

Sponge

Crab

Sponge

Find

When you next visit a beach, try to find a rock pool. Write a list of what you see.

Are there schools in the sea?

Some fish live in big groups called schools. This may protect them from hungry hunters. There are thousands of different types of fish in the sea. Most are covered in shiny scales and use fins and tails to swim. Fish have gills that take in oxygen from the water so that they can breathe.

School of fish

Read

What is a big group of fish called? Read this page to find out.

Which fish looks like an oar?

The oarfish does — and it can grow to be as long as four canoes! It is the longest bony fish and is found in all the world's oceans. Oarfish have a bright red fin along the length of their back. They swim upright through the water.

Oarfish

Flying high
Fish can't survive out of water for long, but flying fish can leap above the waves when swimming at high speed. They look like they are flying as they use their fins to glide through the air.

Sunfish

Do fish like to sunbathe?

Sunfish like sunbathing. Ocean sunfish are huge fish that can weigh up to one tonne — as heavy as a small car! They swim at the surface, as if they're sunbathing.

What is the scariest shark?

Great whites are the scariest sharks. These huge fish speed through the water at 30 kilometres an hour. Unlike most fish, the great white shark has warm blood. This allows its muscles to work well but it also means that it needs to eat lots of meat. Great white sharks are fierce hunters. They will attack and eat almost anything, but prefer to feed on seals.

Great white shark

When is a whale not a whale?

When it is an orca. Killer whales are also called orcas – they are the biggest member of the dolphin family. Killer whales will kill and eat almost anything in the ocean from a small fish or seabird, to a large whale.

Killer whale attacking a sea lion

Yum yum!

Most sharks are meat eaters. Herring are a favourite food for sand tiger and thresher sharks, while a hungry tiger shark will gobble up just about anything!

When is a shark like a pup?

When it's a baby. Young sharks are called pups. Some grow inside their mother's body. Others hatch from eggs straight into the sea.

Draw

Using felt-tip pens, draw your own underwater picture. Include a great white shark.

Who builds walls beneath the sea?

Tiny animals build underwater walls. These walls are made of coral, the leftover skeletons of tiny sea animals called polyps. Over millions of years, enough skeletons pile up to form walls. These make a coral reef. All kinds of creatures live around a reef.

Parrotfish

Seahorse

Clownfish

LOOK
Do you know where the Great Barrier Reef is? Look carefully in an atlas to find out.

How do fish keep clean?

Cleaner wrasse are little fish that help other fish to keep clean! Larger fish, such as groupers and moray eels, visit the cleaner wrasse, which nibble all the bugs and bits of dirt off the bigger fishes' bodies — what a feast!

Super reef
You can see the Great Barrier Reef from space! At over 2000 kilometres long, it is the largest thing ever built by living creatures.

Lionfish

Coral reef

Cleaner wrasse fish

When is a fish like a clown?

When it's a clownfish. These fish are brightly coloured, like circus clowns. They live among the stinging arms (tentacles) of the sea anemone, where they are safe from enemies.

Sea anemone

113

Why are whales so big?

Whales have grown to such a huge size because they live in water. The water helps to support their enormous bulk. The blue whale is the biggest animal in the ocean – and the whole planet. It is about 30 metres long and can weigh up to 150 tonnes. Every day, it eats about four tonnes of tiny, shrimp-like creatures called krill.

Blue whale

Can whales sing songs?

All whales make sounds, such as squeaks and moans. The male humpback whale seems to sing, probably to attract a mate. He may repeat his song for up to 20 hours!

Humpback whale

Stick around!
Barnacles are shellfish. They attach themselves to ships, or the bodies of grey whales and other large sea animals.

Measure
The blue whale is 30 metres long. Can you measure how long you are?

Do whales grow tusks?

The narwhal has a tusk like a unicorn's. This tusk is a long, twirly tooth that comes out of the whale's head. The males use their tusks as weapons when they fight over females. The tusk can grow to 3 metres in length.

Do lions live in the sea?

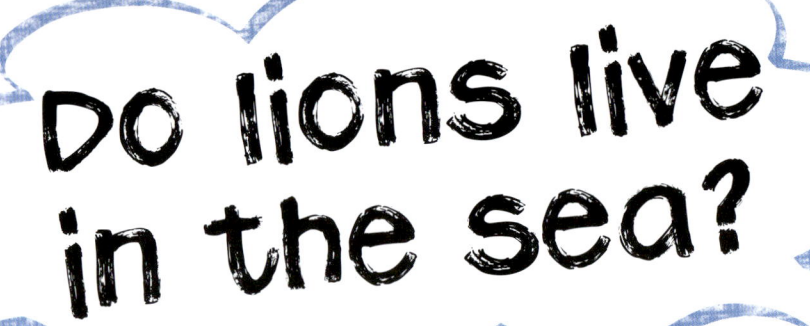

There are lions in the sea, but not the furry, roaring kind. Sea lions, seals and walruses are all warm-blooded animals that have adapted to ocean life. They have flippers instead of legs – far more useful for swimming. A thick layer of fat under the skin keeps them warm in cold water.

Think
What do you think whales, dolphins and seals have in common with humans?

Seals

Who can crack open shellfish?

Sea otters can! They balance a rock on their tummy while floating on their back, and crack the shellfish open by banging it on the rock.

Sea otter

Singing seal!
Leopard seals sing in their sleep! These seals, found in the Antarctic, chirp and whistle while they snooze.

Can a walrus change colour?

Walruses seem to change colour. In cold water, a walrus can look pale brown or even white. This is because blood drains from the skin to stop the body losing heat. On land, blood returns to the skin and the walrus looks pink!

Are there crocodiles in the sea?

Most crocodiles live in rivers and swamps. The saltwater crocodile also swims out to sea — it doesn't seem to mind the salty water. These crocodiles are huge, and can grow to be 7 metres long and one tonne in weight.

Saltwater crocodile

Find
Turtles only come ashore for one reason. Can you do some research and find out why?

Which lizard loves to swim?

Most lizards live on land, where it is easier to warm up their cold-blooded bodies. Marine iguanas depend on the sea for food and dive underwater to eat seaweed. When they are not diving, they sit on rocks to soak up the sunshine.

Marine iguana

How deep can a turtle dive?

Leatherback turtles can dive up to 1200 metres for their dinner. They are the biggest sea turtles and they make the deepest dives. Leatherbacks feed mostly on jellyfish but also eat crabs, lobsters and starfish.

Leatherback turtles

Slithery snakes

There are poisonous snakes in the sea. The banded sea snake and the yellow-bellied sea snake both use poison to kill their prey. Their poison is far stronger than that of land snakes.

Do seabirds dig burrows?

Most seabirds make nests on cliffs. The puffin digs a burrow on the clifftop, like a rabbit. Sometimes, a puffin even takes over an empty rabbit hole. Here it lays its egg. Both parents look after the chick when it hatches.

Think
Sea birds have webbed feet. Why do you think this is? Do you have webbed feet?

Puffins

Wandering albatross

Can seabirds sleep as they fly?

Wandering albatrosses are the biggest seabirds and spend months at sea. They are very good gliders, and even sleep as they fly. To feed, they sit on the surface of the water and catch creatures such as squid. An albatross has a wingspan of around 3 metres – about the length of a family car!

Hop on over

The smallest seabird is the Wilson's storm petrel, at just 16 to 19 centimetres long. It is found over the Atlantic, Indian and Antarctic Oceans. This petrel hops over the water's surface, snatching tiny sea creatures to eat.

Which birds like to dance?

Boobies are seabirds that live in large groups. The males have bright red or blue feet. When they are looking for a mate, they dance in front of the female, to attract her with their colourful feet!

Blue-footed booby

How do polar bears learn to swim?

Polar bears are good swimmers and they live around the freezing Arctic Ocean. They learn to swim when they are cubs, by following their mother into the water. With their big front paws, the bears paddle through the water. They can swim for many hours.

Polar bear

Imagine
Pretend to be a polar bear. Imagine what life is like at the North Pole.

Are penguins fast swimmers?

Penguins are birds — but they cannot fly. All penguins are fast swimmers. The fastest swimmer is the gentoo penguin. It can reach speeds of 27 kilometres an hour underwater.

Gentoo penguin

Small and tall!
The smallest penguin is the fairy penguin at just 40 centimetres tall. The biggest is the emperor penguin at 1.3 metres in height — as tall as a seven-year-old child!

Emperor penguins

Which penguin dad likes to babysit?

Emperor penguin dads look after the chicks. The female lays an egg and leaves her mate to keep it warm. The male balances the egg on his feet to keep it off the ice. He goes without food until the chick hatches. When it does, the mother returns and both parents care for it.

Is seaweed good to eat?

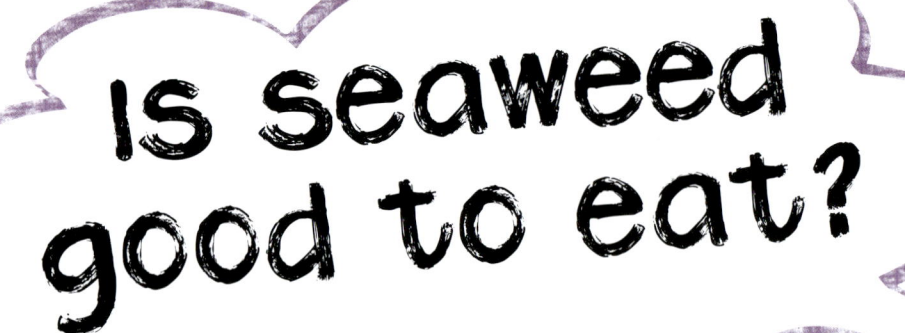

Seaweed can be very good to eat. In shallow, warm seawater, people can grow their own seaweed. It is then dried in the sun, which helps to keep it fresh. Seaweed is even used to make ice cream!

Collecting seaweed

List
Make a list of the things you can eat from the ocean. Which foods have you tried before?

How do we get salt from the sea?

Sea water is salty. Salt is an important substance. In hot, low-lying areas, people build walls to hold shallow pools of sea water. The water dries up in the sun, leaving behind crystals of salt.

How are lobsters caught?

Lobsters are large, edible shellfish. Fishermen catch them in wooden cages called pots. Attracted to dead fish put in the pots, lobsters push the door of the pot open to reach the fish. But once inside, the lobster can't get out again.

Lobster pot

Pearly oysters

Pearls grow inside oysters. If a grain of sand gets stuck in an oyster's shell, it irritates it. The oyster slowly coats the grain with a substance that is used to line the inside of its shell. As more coats are added, a pearl forms.

Are there chimneys under the sea?

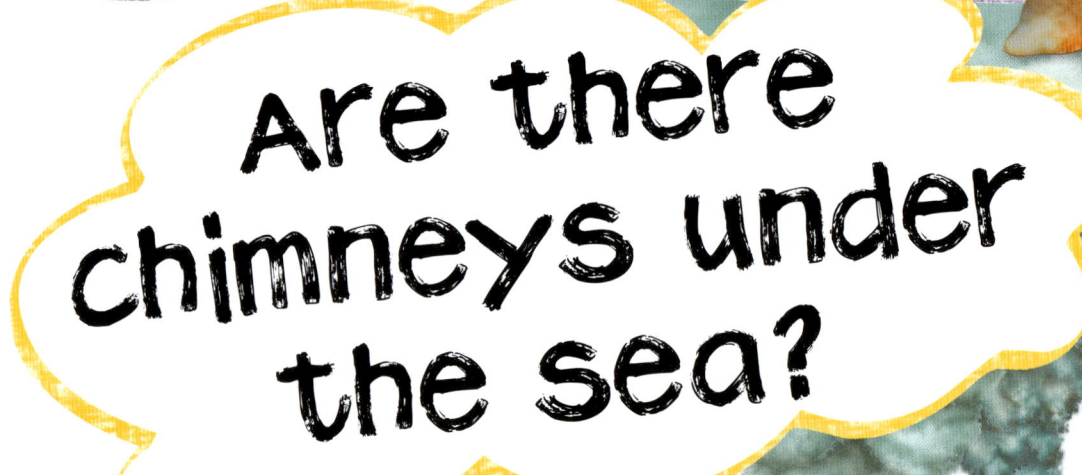

Rocky chimneys on the ocean floor give off clouds of hot water. These chimneys lie deep beneath the ocean. The hot water feeds strange creatures, such as tube worms and sea spiders.

Rat tail fish

Giant clams

Watery village
In 1963, diver Jacques Cousteau built a village on the bed of the Red Sea. Along with four other divers, he lived there for a whole month.

Do monsters live in the sea?

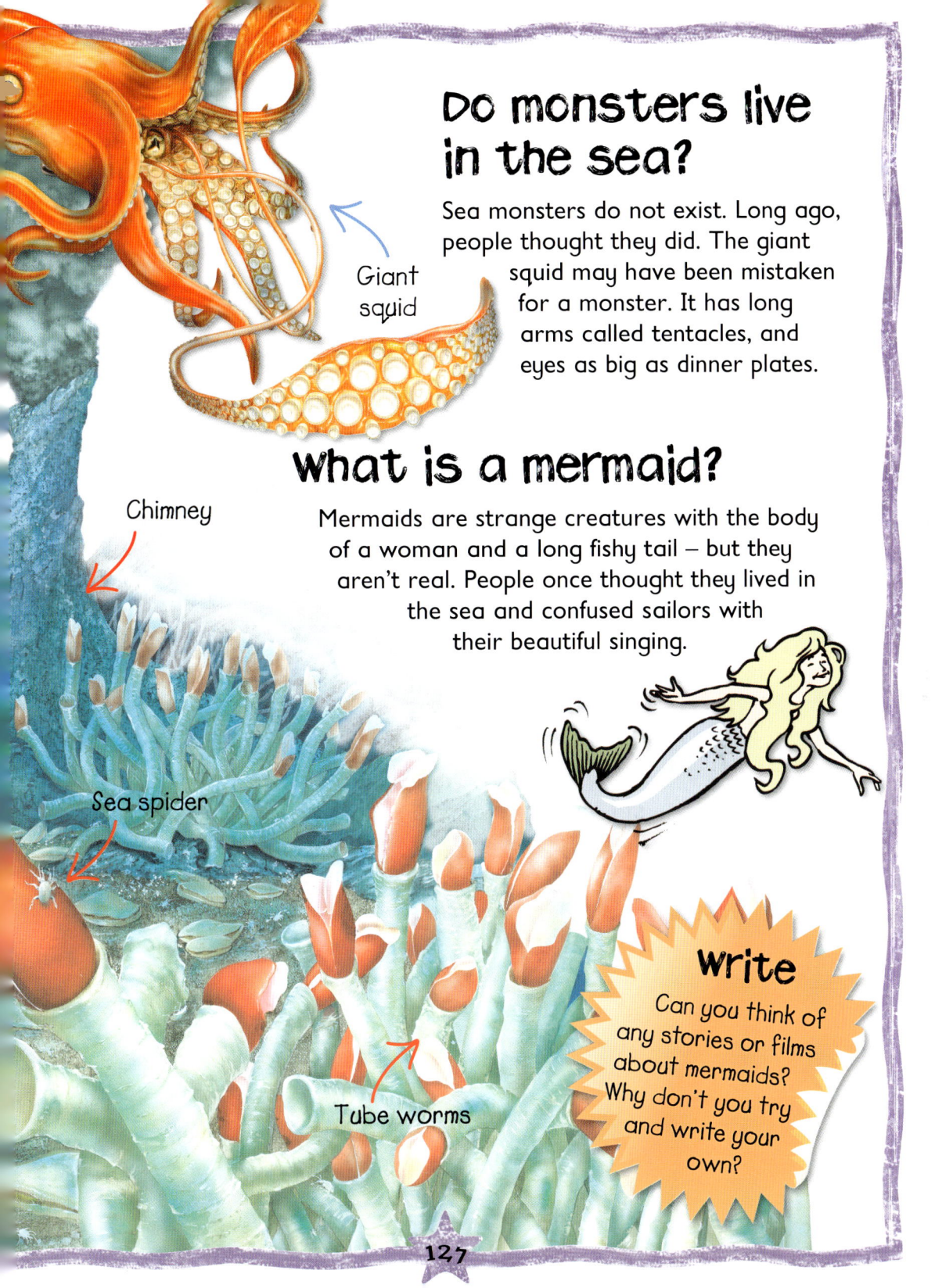

Sea monsters do not exist. Long ago, people thought they did. The giant squid may have been mistaken for a monster. It has long arms called tentacles, and eyes as big as dinner plates.

Giant squid

What is a mermaid?

Mermaids are strange creatures with the body of a woman and a long fishy tail – but they aren't real. People once thought they lived in the sea and confused sailors with their beautiful singing.

Chimney

Sea spider

Tube worms

Write
Can you think of any stories or films about mermaids? Why don't you try and write your own?

How do divers breathe underwater?

Divers have a spare pair of lungs. Scuba divers carry a special piece of breathing equipment called an 'aqua lung'. These are tanks filled with oxygen (air) that sit on the divers' backs. A long tube supplies the diver with air.

Aqua lung

Diver

Wear
Try wearing some goggles in the bath. Pop in some toys and see what they look like under the water.

What is a jetski?

A jetski is like a motorbike without wheels that travels on water. It pushes out a jet of water behind it, which pushes it forward. Some jetskiers can reach speeds of 100 kilometres an hour.

Jetski

Can people ride the waves?

Yes they can, on surfboards. Surfing became popular in the 1950s. Modern surfboards are made of super-light material. People stand up on their surfboards and ride the waves. The best places to surf are off the coasts of Mexico and Hawaii.

Surfer

Water record!

A single boat towed 100 waterskiers! This record was made off the coast of Australia in 1986 and no one has beaten it yet. The drag boat was a cruiser called 'Reef Cat'.

Quiz time

Do you remember what you have read about oceans? Here are some questions to test your memory. The pictures will help you. If you get stuck, read the pages again.

1. Are there volcanoes under the sea?

page 105

2. When is a sponge like an animal?

page 107

page 109

3. Which fish looks like an oar?

4. When is a whale not a whale?

page 111

page 115

5. Do whales grow tusks?

page 117

6. Who can crack open shellfish?

7. Are there crocodiles in the sea?

page 124

page 118

11. Is seaweed good to eat?

8. Can seabirds sleep as they fly?

12. What is a mermaid?

page 127

page 121

page 128

9. How do polar bears learn to swim?

13. How do divers breathe underwater?

page 122

page 123

10. Which penguin dad likes to babysit?

Answers

1. Yes, there are
2. A sponge is an animal
3. The oarfish
4. When it's a killer whale, which is actually a member of the dolphin family
5. Yes, the narwhal has a tusk
6. The sea otter
7. The saltwater crocodile swims in the sea
8. Yes, the wandering albatross can
9. By following their mother into the water
10. The emperor penguin
11. Yes, it can be
12. A creature that is half-woman, half-fish
13. By using an aqua lung

132

Plants

what is a plant?

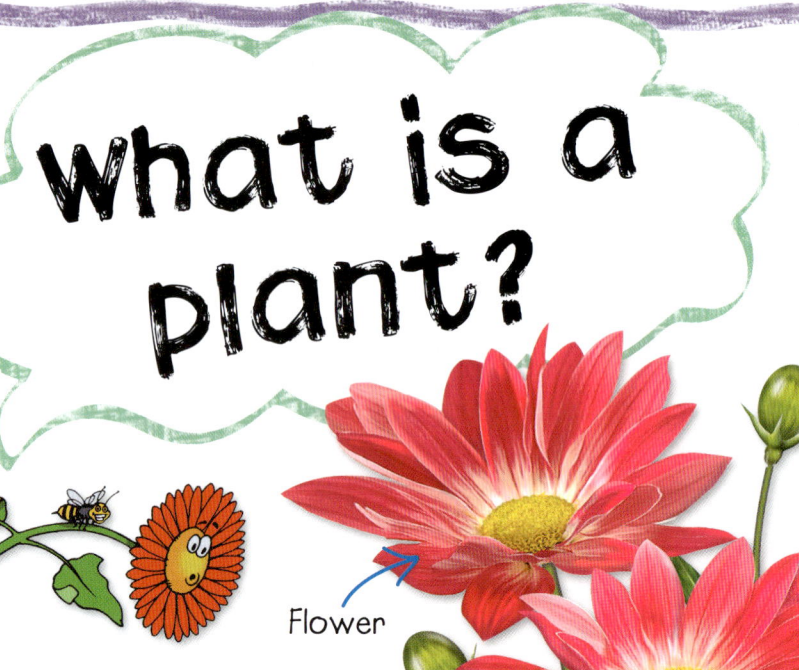

Bud

Flower

A plant is a living thing that breathes, grows and changes. Plants live all over the world, even in deserts, on mountains and underwater. Most plants have flowers, leaves, stems and roots.

Leaf

Stem

Roots

Do bananas grow on trees?

No, but bananas do grow on plants that are almost as tall as trees. A banana plant has one main stem and one big flower. A single bunch of bananas grows from the flower.

Bananas

Potato bug

Big animals eat plants, but so do little ones! Bugs, slugs and mini-beasts all enjoy nibbling fruits, shoots, roots and leaves.

Make

Ask a grown up to help you make a milkshake. You need ice cream, bananas and milk.

Did dinosaurs eat plants?

Some dinosaurs feasted on meat, but the biggest ones munched on plants. They probably spent all day eating to get enough energy for their giant bodies to keep moving!

Why do flowers like bees?

Bee collecting pollen

Flowers like bees, and bees like flowers! Bees help flowers to grow seeds, and flowers give bees food. Look at a flower and you will see a yellow dust, called pollen. Bees eat pollen, and collect it to take back to their hives.

Seedlings

Can plants move?

Plants don't have arms, legs or wings, but they can still move. All plants need sunlight, and they can bend their stems so their leaves face the Sun.

Grow
Grow some cress seedlings. Look at how the seedlings bend towards the light as they grow.

Pollen coat
Bats are flying animals that come out at night. They feed on flower nectar and can get covered in pollen!

Who knocks nuts?

Birds called nutcrackers do! Nuts are seeds with hard shells. Nutcrackers open nuts by bashing them against rocks. The hard shells fall away, and the bird can eat the seed inside.

How tall can a tree grow?

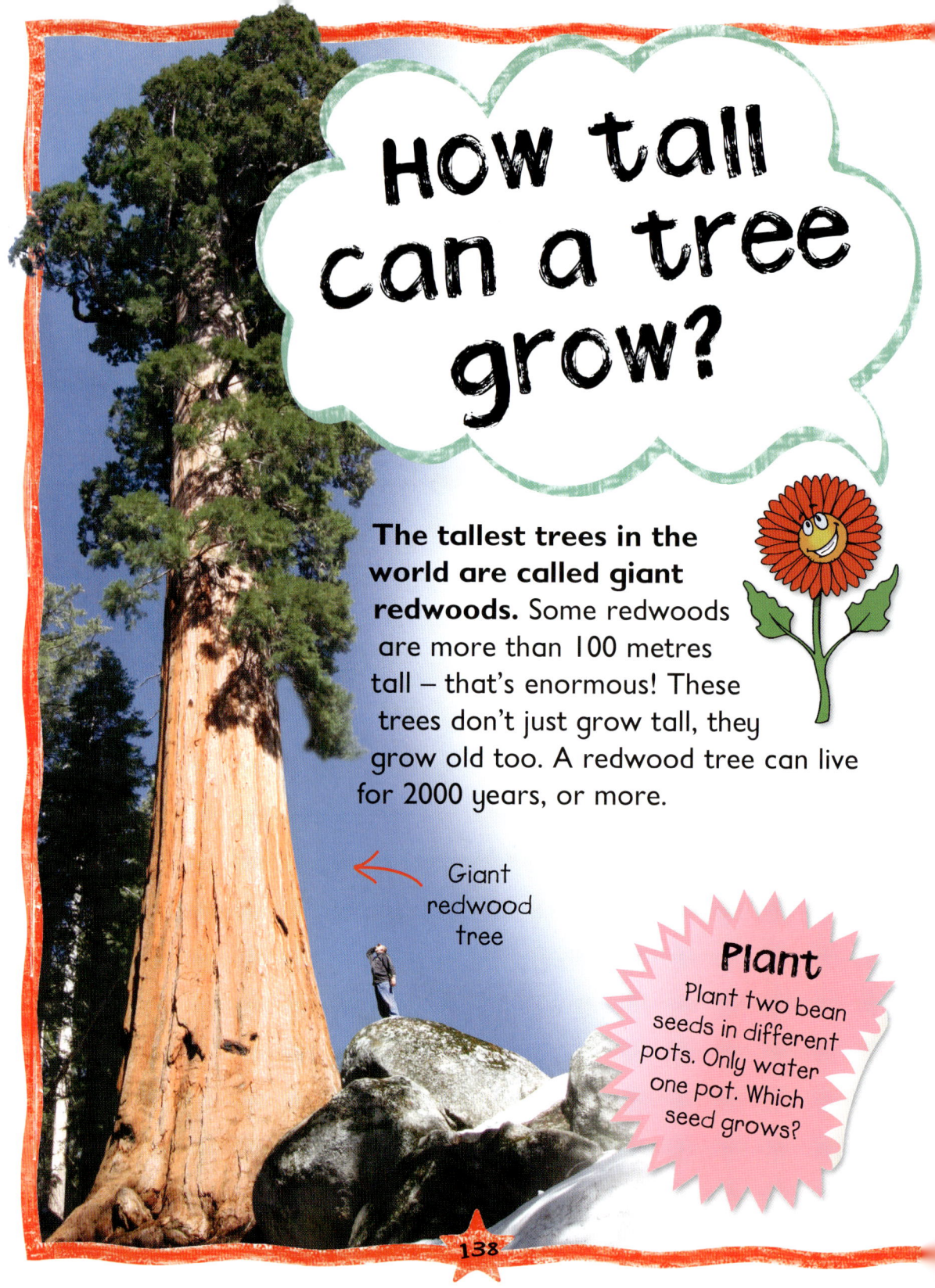

The tallest trees in the world are called giant redwoods. Some redwoods are more than 100 metres tall — that's enormous! These trees don't just grow tall, they grow old too. A redwood tree can live for 2000 years, or more.

← Giant redwood tree

Plant
Plant two bean seeds in different pots. Only water one pot. Which seed grows?

why do hummingbirds hum?

Tiny hummingbirds beat their wings so fast, they make a humming sound. These birds also hover – when they beat their wings they stay in one place. This means they can drink nectar from a flower without having to land on it.

Sweet smell

Rose petals have a lovely scent. Long ago, ladies put petals in their bath water to make it smell lovely.

Cacti

can plants live in a desert?

Yes they can. Plants need water to live, but it doesn't often rain in a desert. Cacti are plants that live in very dry places, and they have tiny spiny leaves. When it rains, cacti save water in their fat stems.

Why do flowers smell nice?

Butterfly feeding on nectar

Flowers smell nice because they want animals to visit them. When a butterfly feeds on a flower's nectar, it picks up pollen on its feet and takes it to another flower. There, the pollen joins with an egg, and grows into a seed.

Which plants can pop?

Squirting cucumbers can squirt their seeds 5 metres away! Their seedpods are full of water, and pop when they are ripe, sending their brown seeds far and wide.

Make
Ask a grown up to make popcorn with you. When the air inside each piece of corn gets hot, it pops!

Do toads sit on toadstools?

Hungry bugs
Caterpillars spend all day eating leaves and growing. They are so hungry that one caterpillar can eat every leaf on a plant.

Toads sometimes sit on toadstools, but they prefer to hide in the damp grass and leaves underneath them. Toadstools and mushrooms are types of fungus. Some fungi are very poisonous.

Toadstools and mushrooms

What is an upside-down tree?

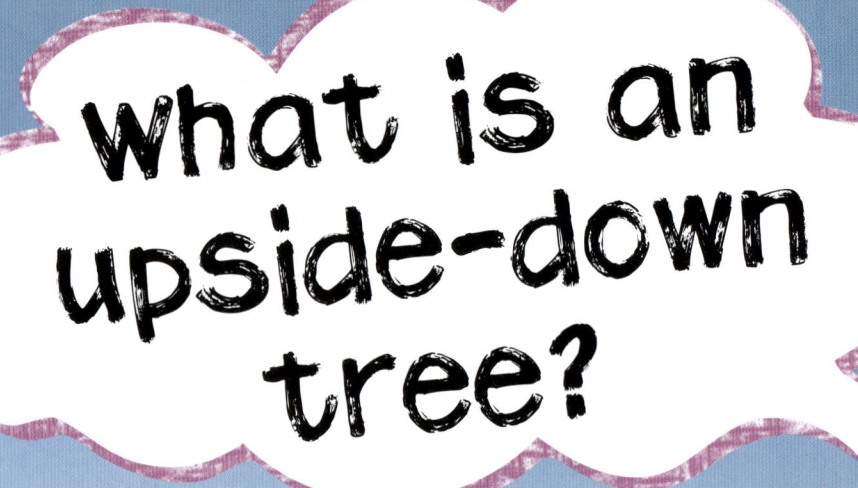

Baobab trees are called upside-down trees. They have big, fat trunks and stumpy little branches that look like roots, especially when their leaves have fallen off. These funny-looking trees grow in Africa.

Baobab trees

Different types of roots

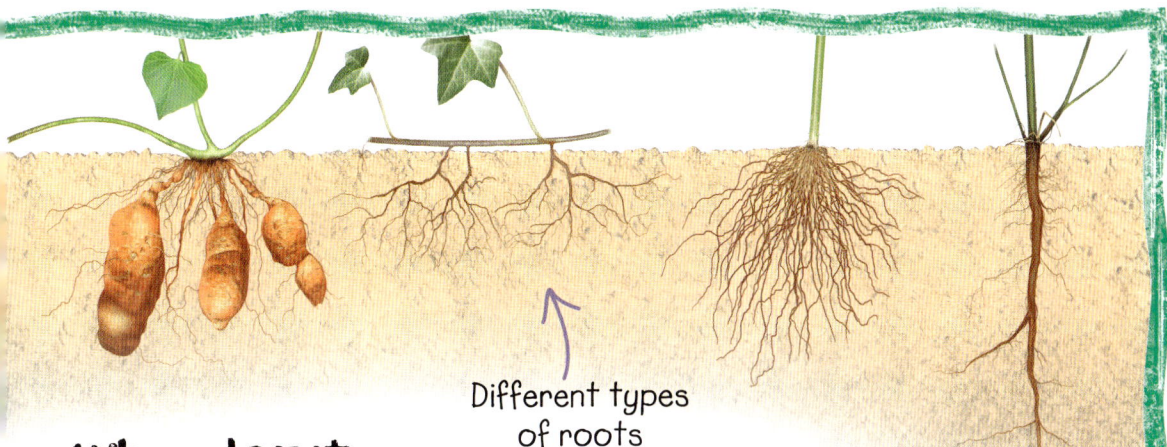

Why don't plants fall over?

Because they have roots. Roots grow into the ground and help to support plants. They suck up water for plants to drink. Roots can be different shapes and sizes. Carrots and sweet potatoes are roots.

Mega roots

Most of the time, we can't see a plant's roots, even though they may be huge. Many plants have roots that are bigger than the rest of the plant.

Which bird pretends to be a tree?

Lots of animals pretend to be plants. Stick insects pretend to be twigs, leaf bugs look like leaves, and potoos are birds that pretend to be dead branches. It's a very good disguise!

Draw

Draw a butterfly feeding on a flower. Use bright paints, crayons or pens to colour it in.

can plants grow on animals?

It's strange to think of plants growing on animals, but it is possible. Sloths live in the jungle. They move so slowly that tiny plants, called algae, grow in their fur. It makes the sloths look green!

Mother and baby sloths

Why are leaves green?

Leaves are green because they are filled with a special green substance, which helps plants to make their food. All plants need sunlight, air and water to make food.

Green leaves

Sun fun
Plants can only make food during the day, when the sun shines. At night they rest, just like we do.

Find
Collect leaves that have different shapes and use them to make some leaf prints. You will need paper and paint.

Why do otters sleep in seaweed?

Sea otters wrap strands of seaweed around themselves so they don't float away. They like to sleep and eat wrapped up like this.

Why do moths need long tongues?

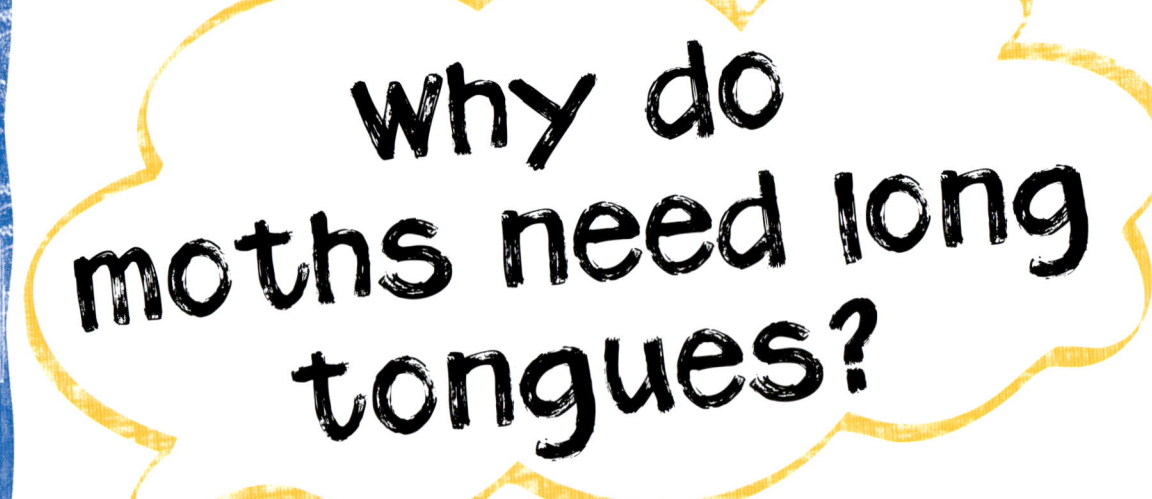

Moths and butterflies need long tongues to reach the nectar deep inside a flower. Nectar is a sugary juice that lots of insects and birds like to drink. It tastes sweet, and it gives them lots of energy too.

Tongue

Moth feeding on nectar

what is the biggest flower?

The world's biggest flower is enormous. It is called a rafflesia, and one bloom can measure up to 100 centimetres wide. Rafflesia flowers have five petals and they grow in rainforests.

Go away!

The spines on a cactus are sharp, little leaves. Plants stop animals from eating them with thorns, spines and even nasty tastes.

Rafflesia flower

Do plants have eyes?

Plants don't have eyes and they cannot see. Sometimes we say that potatoes have 'eyes', but these are just the places where roots and stems are starting to grow.

Measure
Use a measuring tape to see how big a rafflesia is. Is it bigger than you?

147

Why are some plants sticky?

Sundew plants are sticky so they can catch flies. When a fly lands on the drops of sugary juice, it soon discovers that its feet are stuck to the plant. Sundew plants catch flies because they like to eat them!

Fly →

← Sundew plant

Why do bluebells grow in spring?

Most plants rest in winter and come to life again in spring. Bluebells, daffodils and tulips all grow in the early spring. They appear as soon as the days begin to get longer, and before trees grow new leaves.

Bluebell

Fire starter
Fires don't just kill plants, they can help them grow. The seeds from giant redwood trees only start to grow after there has been a forest fire.

Make!
Ask a grown up to help you make a fruit salad using lots of different fruits.

Does spaghetti grow on trees?

No, but it does come from a plant. Spaghetti and bread are made from wheat, which is a plant that grows in almost every country of the world.

How do ants protect trees?

Ants protect trees by biting animals that try to eat the leaves. In Africa, cows like to eat acacia trees, where ants live and build their nests. When a cow tries to nibble the tasty leaves, the ants run over and bite it!

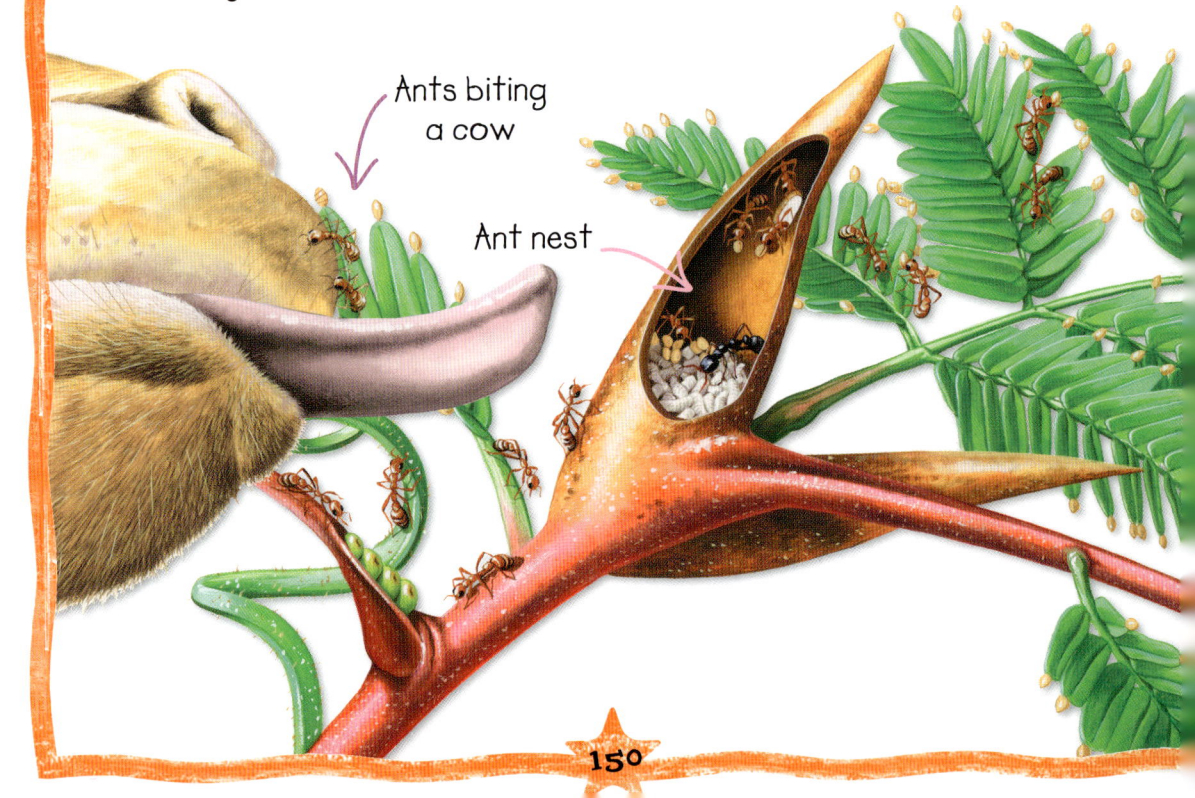

Ants biting a cow

Ant nest

Shake it!
Some plants have smart ways to stay alive. If there has not been enough rain, quiver trees drop entire branches.

Can plants live underwater?

Yes, plants can live underwater as long as sunlight can still reach them. Seaweeds are plants that live underwater in oceans. They look different from other plants and have thick rubbery leaves, which are called fronds.

Seaweed

Where does paper come from?

Bake
Flour comes from a plant called wheat. Bake some biscuits, bread or cakes using flour.

Paper comes from trees. When trees are cut down to make paper, many animals lose their homes. Nearly half of all trees that are cut down in the world are used to make paper.

151

Why do lizards lick flowers?

Most lizards eat bugs, but some of them feed on flowers. This blue-tailed day lizard licks a flower to reach the nectar inside. By doing this, the lizard also helps to transfer pollen to other flowers.

Blue-tailed day lizard

who lives in a tree house?

Some people who live in rainforests live in tree houses. They build their homes at the top of trees. Tree houses keep people safe from their enemies, and from deadly animals.

Super grass

Billions of animals eat grass. They are called grazing animals. Sheep, horses, zebras and rabbits are grazing animals.

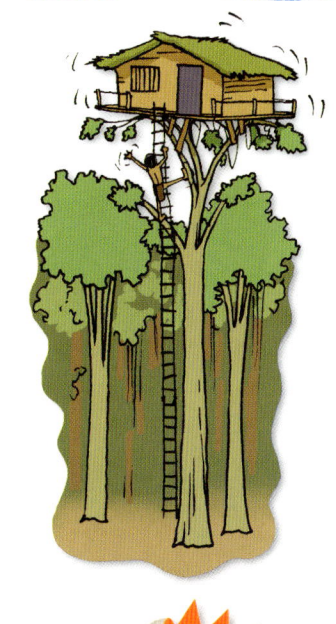

Think
Make up a story about some children who live in a tree house.

Do needles grow on trees?

Yes they do! The long, thin leaves that grow on pine trees are called needles. Pine trees live in cold places, and their seeds grow in cones. Most trees lose leaves in autumn, but pine trees keep theirs all year.

Pine needles

Pine cone

Why do leaves turn red?

At the end of the summer, leaves begin to die. As they die, their colours turn from green to red, gold and brown, before they fall from the tree. This time is called autumn. During winter, the trees will rest, but they are still alive.

Trees in autumn

How do seeds grow?

When the time is right, seeds begin to grow into new plants. They need water, air and warmth to grow. First, a small, white root grows. Then, a new green shoot grows up to the light. Soon, new green leaves grow too.

Leaves

Seed

Green shoot

Find

Go on a nature hunt in autumn. Ask a grown up to help you find colourful leaves, berries, conkers and acorns.

Which tree can you drink from?

In remote places in Australia, native people drink from the paperbark tree if water is scarce. The trunk is full of sweet liquid that is safe to drink.

Brrrrrrr!

Trees and plants don't feel the cold, like we do, but very frosty weather can kill plants.

Why do plants have teeth?

Venus flytrap

A Venus flytrap is a plant that has spikes on its leaves. The spikes look like teeth, and the leaves close like snapping traps. When a fly lands on the trap, it snaps shut and holds the fly inside. Then the plant can begin to eat the tasty fly!

What happens underground?

Plants grow in soil, which is full of tiny animals. Some of these bugs and worms eat roots, but most of them help to make the soil a healthy place for plants.

Fussy koalas

Koalas only eat leaves from gum trees. They spend up to 22 hours every day fast asleep, and eat for the rest of the time.

How do birds help plants?

Birds eat berries and fruits from plants. When a bird eats a fruit, the seed inside passes through its body and comes out in its poo. This seed may grow into a new plant.

Bird eating berries

Dig

Ask a grown up to choose a plant to dig up. Can you find any bugs in the soil around the roots?

Which seeds can hitch a ride?

Seeds with prickles can hitch a ride. Grazing animals often walk through plants that have prickly seeds. The prickles can hook onto the animal's fur. The seeds fall off later, and may grow into new plants.

Sheep with prickles in its fur

Prickly seed

158

Can grass grow as tall as trees?

Bamboo is a type of grass. It grows very fast – up to 30 centimetres in just one day! In Asia, there are bamboo forests where each plant grows as tall as a tree. Bamboo stems are hollow, and they can bend in the wind without breaking.

Healthy veg

We need to eat plants to be healthy. Fruit and vegetables are full of vitamins, which help us to grow and stay well.

Bamboo forest

What is a rainforest?

Rainforests are big, thick forests that grow in hot places. It rains almost every day in a rainforest. These forests are special because so many different types of animals and plants live in them.

Measure

If a plant grows 10 centimetres in one day, how much will it grow in one week?

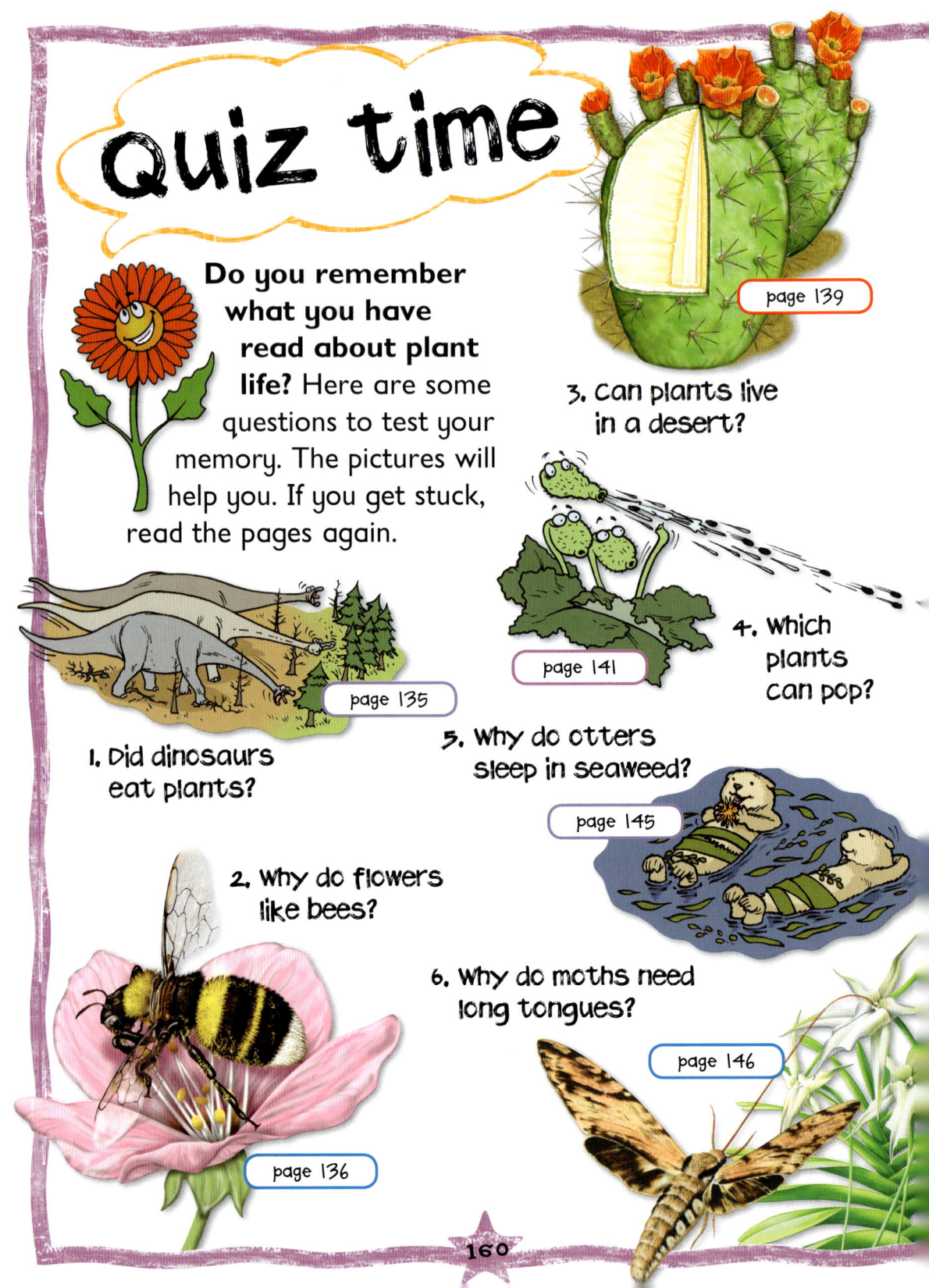

Quiz time

Do you remember what you have read about plant life? Here are some questions to test your memory. The pictures will help you. If you get stuck, read the pages again.

3. Can plants live in a desert?
page 139

4. Which plants can pop?
page 141

1. Did dinosaurs eat plants?
page 135

5. Why do otters sleep in seaweed?
page 145

2. Why do flowers like bees?
page 136

6. Why do moths need long tongues?
page 146

160

7. Do plants have eyes?
page 147

8. Why do bluebells grow in spring?
page 149

9. Where does paper come from?
page 151

10. Why do lizards lick flowers?
page 152

11. Who lives in a tree house?
page 153

12. Which tree can you drink from?
page 155

13. How do birds help plants?
page 157

Answers

1. Yes, lots of dinosaurs ate plants
2. Because bees help flowers to grow seeds
3. Yes, cacti are plants that live in deserts
4. Squirting cucumbers pop
5. To stop themselves floating away
6. To reach nectar deep inside flowers
7. No, but potatoes have places called 'eyes' where roots and stems start to grow
8. Because the days begin to grow longer
9. Paper comes from trees
10. To eat the nectar inside
11. Some rainforest people live in tree houses
12. The paperbark tree
13. By eating berries and fruits, birds can help new plants to spread and grow

161

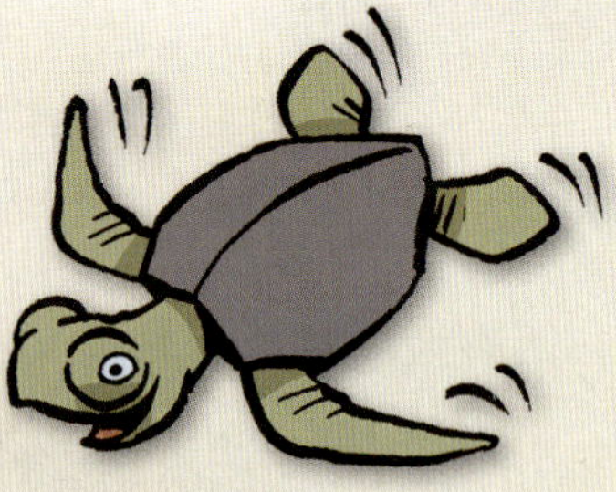

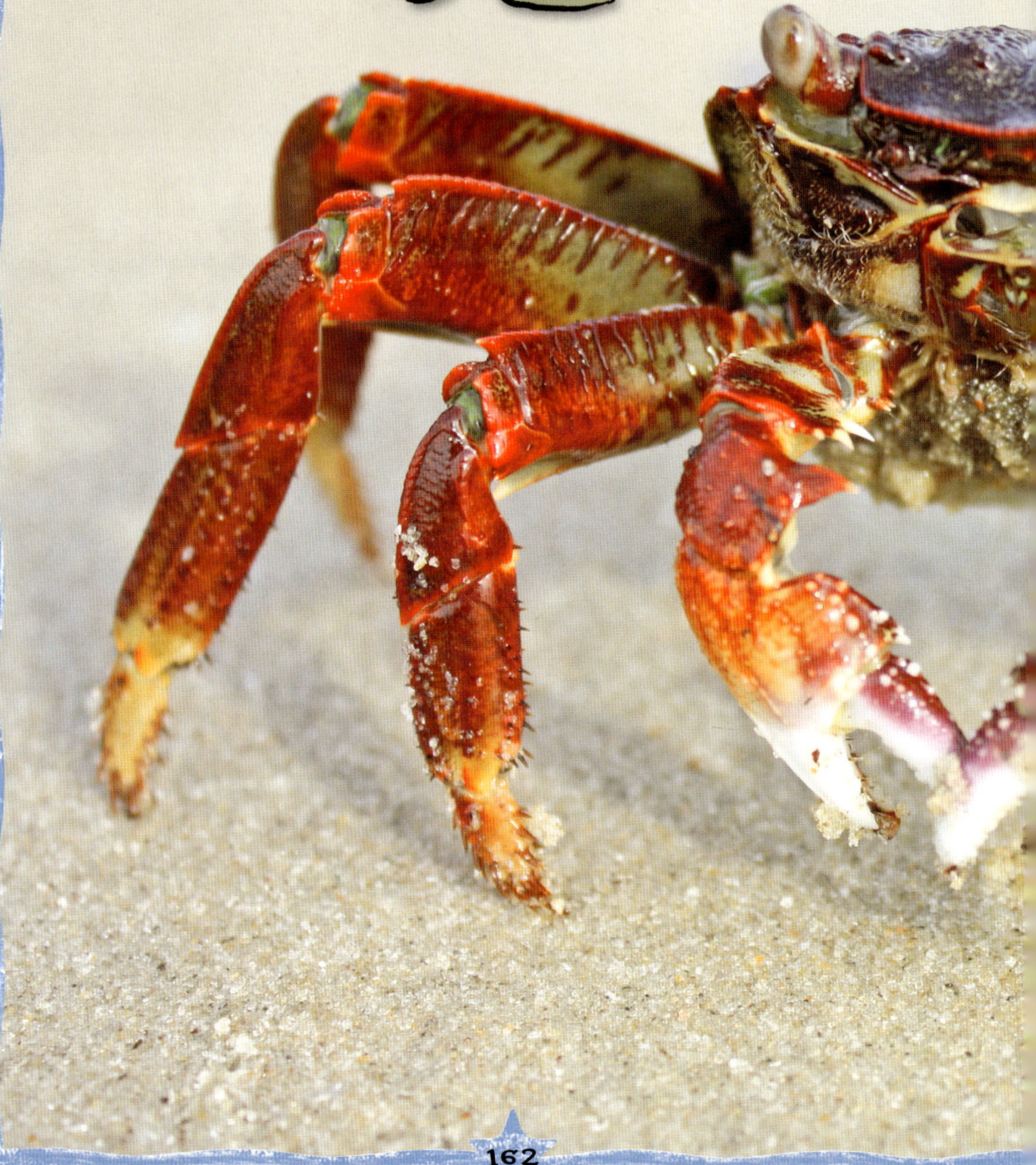

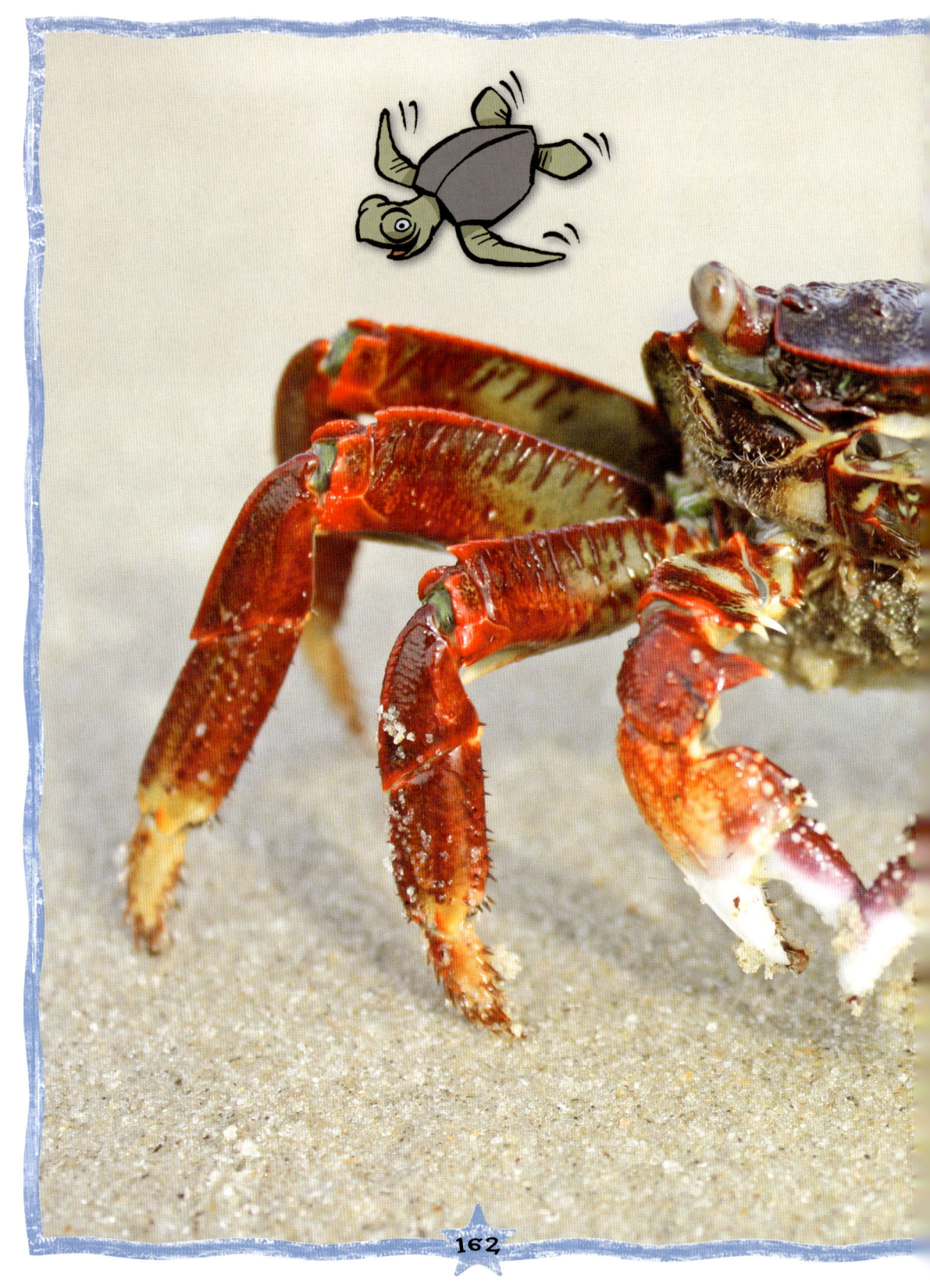

Seashore

How long is the seashore?

Around the world there are thousands of kilometres of seashore. It can be sandy, pebbly, muddy, or rocky with high cliffs. Many interesting plants and animals make their homes on or near the shore – and so do millions of people.

Sandy seashore

Which shores are the coldest?

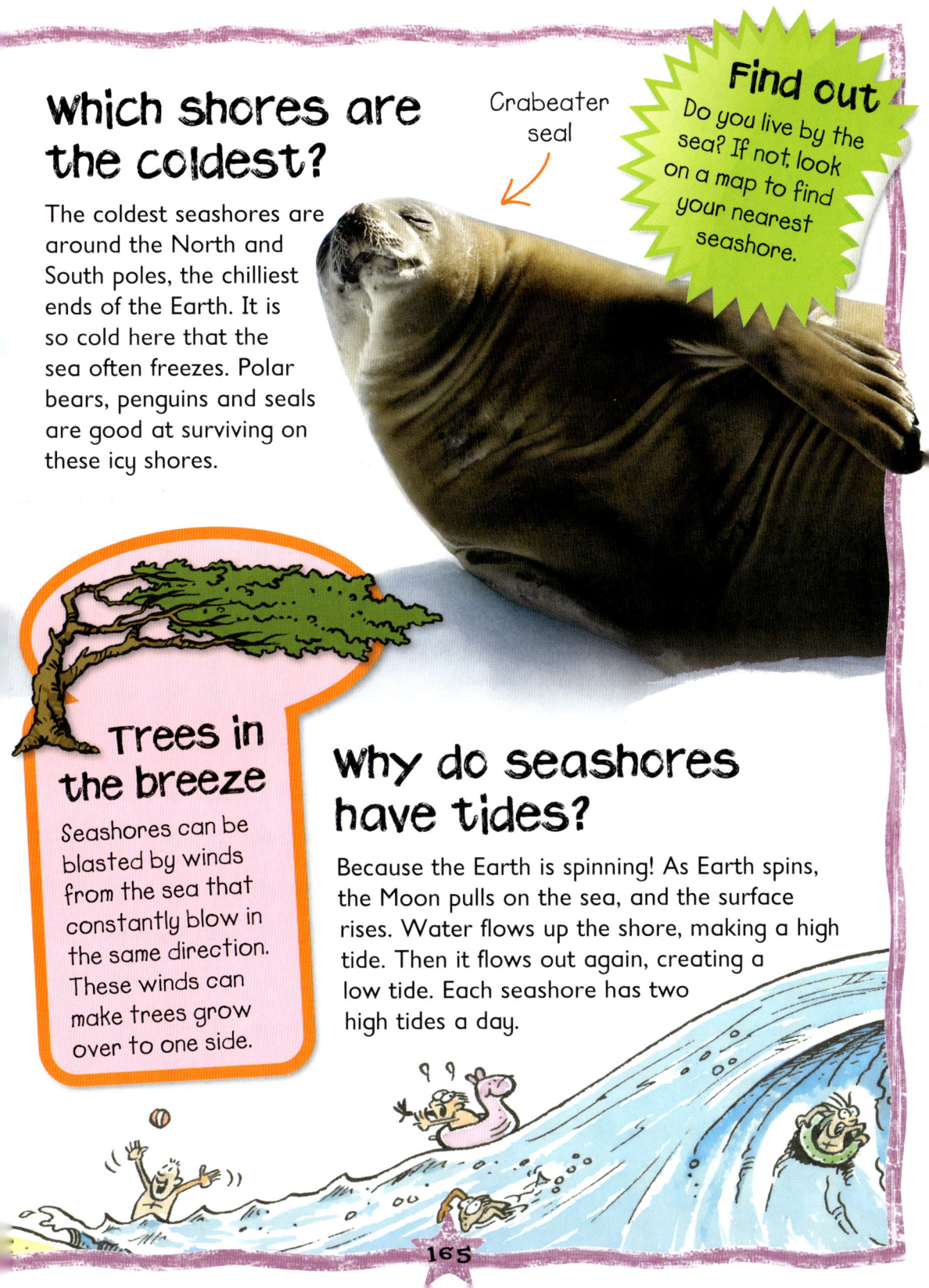

Crabeater seal

The coldest seashores are around the North and South poles, the chilliest ends of the Earth. It is so cold here that the sea often freezes. Polar bears, penguins and seals are good at surviving on these icy shores.

Find out
Do you live by the sea? If not, look on a map to find your nearest seashore.

Trees in the breeze
Seashores can be blasted by winds from the sea that constantly blow in the same direction. These winds can make trees grow over to one side.

Why do seashores have tides?

Because the Earth is spinning! As Earth spins, the Moon pulls on the sea, and the surface rises. Water flows up the shore, making a high tide. Then it flows out again, creating a low tide. Each seashore has two high tides a day.

Why do seashells cling to rocks?

They cling to rocks so they don't get washed away by the tide. Animals such as limpets, mussels and barnacles live inside seashells. At high tide they open their shells to find food. At low tide, the shells shut tight so they don't dry out.

Limpet

Barnacles

Mussels

write
When you next visit a sandy beach, try writing your name in the sand with a stick.

What are seashore zones?

The area between high and low tide is called the intertidal zone. Low tide zone is wettest, and has lots of seaweed. High tide zone is drier, and has more land plants.

Fun at the beach
Sandy beaches make a great place for sports, such as horseriding, kite-flying, football and volleyball.

How big are the biggest waves?

Winds make waves, which break onto the seashore. Some waves can be 30 metres high — taller than a tower of 18 people. The biggest waves are tsunamis, caused by earthquakes shaking the sea.

What is a coral reef?

A coral reef is a stony structure found in shallow oceans. Tiny animals called polyps build up layers of hard, colourful coral over many years, to use as a home. A reef also makes a good home for other sea creatures, such as fish, rays, octopuses, turtles and crabs.

Coral reef

Why do crabs walk sideways?

If crabs want to move quickly, walking sideways is best! Their flat, wide bodies help them slip into narrow hiding places. This means that their legs only bend sideways. Crabs can walk forwards, but only very slowly.

Sharks in the shallows

Some sharks, like the black-tip reef shark, are often found swimming around coral reefs in search of a snack.

Do all crabs have shells?

Most crabs have a hard shell, but hermit crabs don't. They need to find some kind of 'shell' to protect their soft bodies. Usually, they use another sea creature's old empty shell.

Christmas Island red crab

Make

Using modelling clay, make a hermit crab and give it a home from a shell, cup or plastic lid.

Why do birds love the seaside?

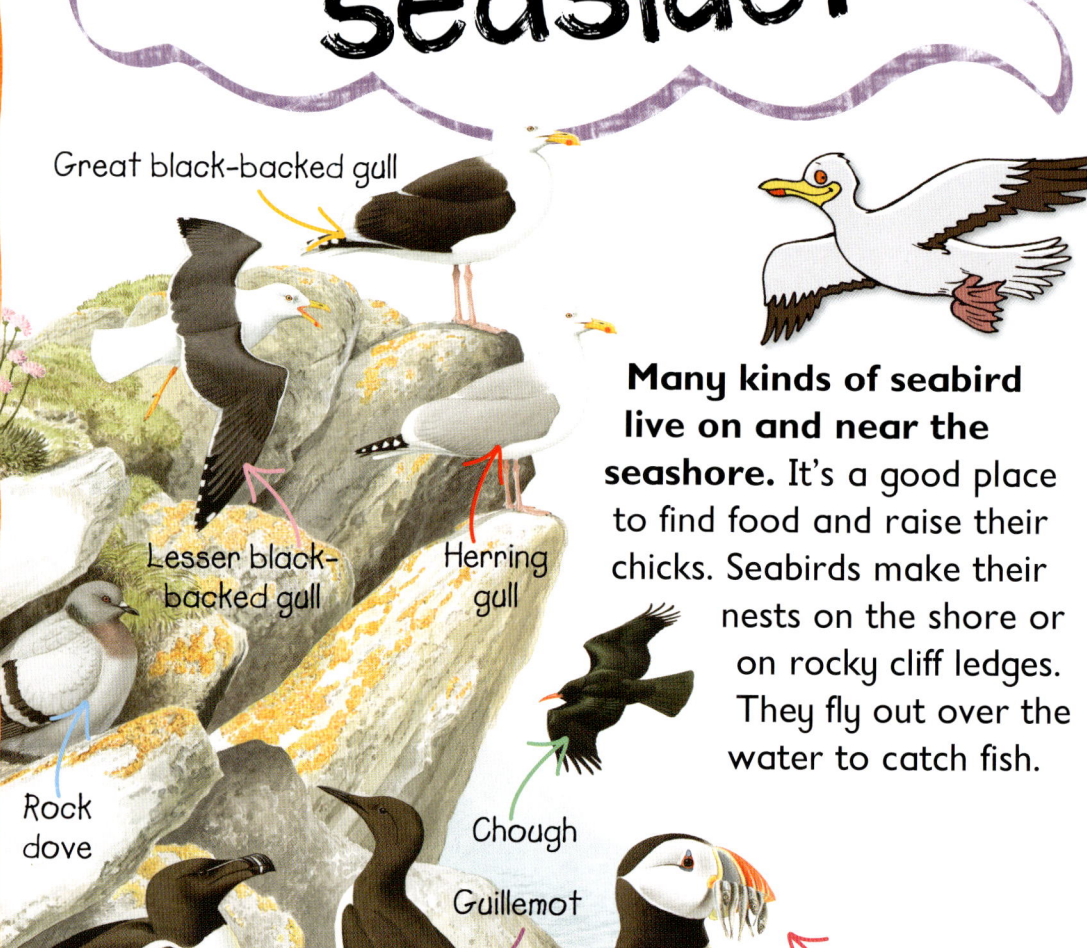

Great black-backed gull

Lesser black-backed gull

Herring gull

Rock dove

Razorbill

Chough

Guillemot

Puffin

Many kinds of seabird live on and near the seashore. It's a good place to find food and raise their chicks. Seabirds make their nests on the shore or on rocky cliff ledges. They fly out over the water to catch fish.

Do beetles head for the beach?

The tiger beetle does! This shiny, green beetle lays its eggs in warm, sandy places. These beetles are often found in sand dunes – small, grassy hills of sand at the top of a beach.

Tiger beetle

Paint
Copy the picture on this page and paint a tiger beetle. Add green glitter for its shiny body.

Swimming cats
Some tigers live in mangrove forests near the coast. They like to splash in the water to cool down.

How does being sick help a chick?

Fulmars are seabirds. When they go fishing, they leave their chicks alone in their nests. If hunting animals come near the nests, the chicks squirt stinky, fishy, oily vomit to scare them away!

Can you tell a pebble from an egg?

Ringed plover

You might not be able to! The ringed plover lays its speckled eggs on pebbly beaches, where they blend in so well they're almost impossible to see. This helps to keep the eggs safe from animals that might eat them.

Eggs

Think
Apart from birds, can you think of any other animals that lay eggs? Use a book to help you.

Which bird hangs its wings out to dry?

The cormorant dives to catch fish. Its feathers soak up the water, making it easier to stay underwater to hunt. After fishing, the cormorant spreads its wings to dry them out.

Cormorant

Elephants of the seashore

'Sea elephants' are actually a type of seal. They are called elephant seals because they have a big droopy nose a bit like a trunk.

How fast can a gannet dive?

Gannets fish by flying above the sea, then plunging down. They fold their wings behind them, making a rocket shape, and can hit the water at 100 kilometres an hour! This lets them dive deep into the water.

Does the seashore have shapes?

Sea stacks   Arch

Yes, seashores have lots of shapes. There are bays, spits, cliffs, archways and towers. They form over many years, as wind and waves batter the coast. Softer rocks get carved away into bays and hollows. Harder rocks last longer, and form sticking-out headlands.

Shingle spit

Shingle beach

Bay

Make
At a pebbly beach, make a sculpture by balancing small pebbles on top of each other in a tower.

Why are pebbles round?

The pebbles on beaches are stones that have been rolled and tumbled around by waves. As they knock together, they lose their sharp corners and edges, and slowly become smooth and round.

Cave

Cliffs

What is sand made of?

Sand is made of tiny pieces of rocks and shells. Larger lumps gradually break down into grains, as the waves crash onto them and make them swirl around.

Delta

Plastic sand

On some beaches, one in every ten sand grains is actually made of plastic. It comes from litter dropped on beaches or thrown from boats.

Sandy beach

Why is a curlew's beak so long?

To find its food buried in the mud, a curlew needs a long, thin beak! It sticks its beak deep into the mud to pick out worms, crabs and insects. A curlew also has long legs to wade in the water.

Curlew

Measure
With a long ruler, mark out one square metre. Try to imagine thousands of seashells living in this area!

Are seashells different shapes?

Yes, they are. A seashell's shape depends on the creature that lives in it, and how it feeds and moves. Spireshells and tower shells are spirals. Clams and cockles have two hinged shells. They open them to feed, or close them to keep safe.

Clam

Tower shell

Common cockle

Painted top shell

Laver spireshell

How do penguins get out of the water?

Penguins can't fly, but they can swim fast underwater, using their wings as flippers. When they want to get out of the sea, they zoom up to the surface and shoot out of the water, landing on the ice.

Crowds of creatures

Some muddy beaches have more then 50,000 tiny shellfish living in each square metre of mud.

Where might you see a bear by the sea?

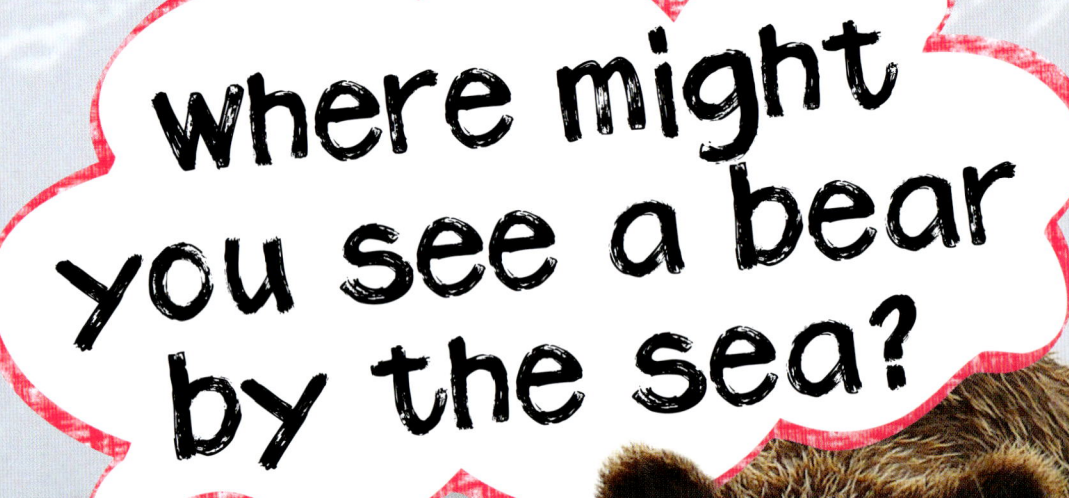

You might see a bear at an estuary, the place where a river meets the sea. In parts of Canada and the United States, grizzly bears try to catch salmon as they leave the sea and head up rivers to breed. They may also nibble berries and sea plants.

Grizzly bear

What is sea pink?

Sea pink is a seashore flower. Not many plants can survive near the sea because it's so windy and salty. But sea pink is tough. It also has special parts that carry salt out of the plant through its leaves.

Sea pink

Down in one

Penguins swallow fish whole, and the fish dissolve inside their stomachs. They can bring the mush back up to feed their chicks.

Why does glass come from the seashore?

Because it's made from sand! Glass is made by heating sand until it melts and turns clear. Long ago, people burnt sea plants such as glasswort to get chemicals for glass-making.

Make

Try some baby penguin food! Mash tinned tuna with a teaspoon of olive oil, and eat it in a sandwich!

What hides in the sand?

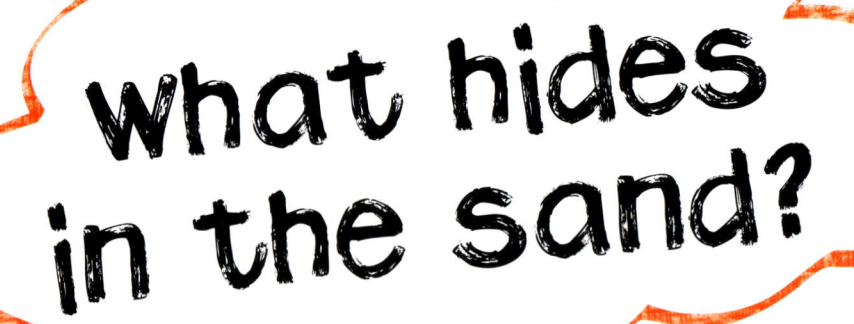

Worms, shrimps, razorshells and some crabs all burrow down into the sand to hide. At high tide they come out and feed. At low tide, being under the sand helps them to stay damp, and avoid being eaten.

Gull

Shrimps

Worms

Razorshell

Hunt
Go on a beach treasure hunt. Look for different shells, different-coloured pebbles and seaweed.

Where is the highest tide in the world?

At the Bay of Fundy in Canada, high tide is super-high! The sea level rises to around 17 metres higher than at low tide. At most beaches, the water is just 2 to 3 metres deeper at high tide.

Treasure-hunting

People love beachcombing too. It's fun to look for interesting creatures, pebbles, shells, or bits of glass that have been rubbed smooth by the sea.

Otter

Lizard

Toad

Which animals go beachcombing?

A line of seaweed, driftwood, shells and litter usually collects at the 'strandline' – the level the high tide flows up to. Seabirds, and other animals such as foxes and otters, go 'beachcombing' along the strandline to look for washed-up crabs and fish to eat.

Crab

what is a lagoon?

A lagoon is a bit like a shallow lake, but filled with salty seawater. They form when part of the sea is surrounded by a sandbar or a coral reef. Lagoons are warm, shallow and protected from storms — so they make great homes for wildlife.

Lagoon

Make
Build your own sandcastle at the beach or in a sandpit. How tall can you make it?

Which fish can walk on land?

Mudskippers are fish, but they can walk on land! They live in the intertidal zone and can breathe in air or water. They skip over the sand or mud, using their front fins like feet.

Mudskipper

Stingers!
Anemones are seashore creatures with stinging tentacles. They grab and sting prey, then gobble it up!

Why do flamingos have long legs?

Flamingos are very tall, pink wading birds. Their long, thin legs help them walk through shallow water in lagoons. They dip their beaks into the water, and use them like a sieve to catch shrimps.

When can you see a rock pool?

When the tide goes out you might see a rock pool. Seawater gets trapped in hollows in rocks or sand. The best places to find rock pools are rocky beaches. Sea creatures shelter here at low tide.

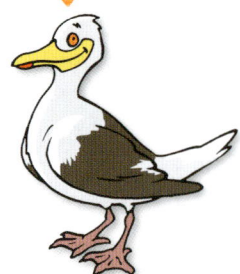

Rock pool

Find out
Compare a photo of a sea anemone with one of an anemone flower. Are they alike?

Are there fleas at the beach?

No, there aren't any fleas, but there are little creatures that look like them. Sandhoppers stay buried in the sand all day, then come out at night to look for food.

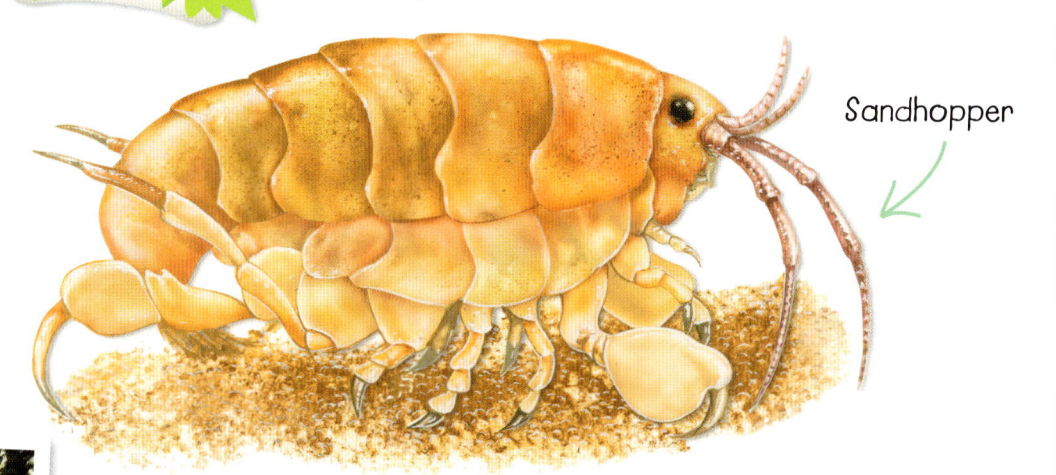

Sandhopper

What lives in a rock pool?

All kinds of creatures live in a rock pool. These can include crabs, sea anemones, sea urchins, shrimps, shellfish, starfish, sponges, small fish and even octopuses. There are also seaweeds, which animals can hide under.

Super sponges
Rock pool sponges are actually simple animals! The natural sponge that you might use in the bath is a long-dead, dried-out sponge!

Which forest grows in the sea?

Mangroves are trees that grow in salty water or seaside mud. Some seashores, especially in hot, tropical places, have mangrove forests growing along them. The mangroves' roots stick out of the ground, and get covered by the tide when it comes in.

Mangroves

Why do crabs turn the ground bright red?

When red crabs march, they turn the ground into a red, moving mass! These crabs live on Christmas Island in the Indian Ocean. Twice a year, thousands of red crabs head to the sea to lay eggs. Then they go back to their forest homes.

Red crabs

Play
Have a crab race with your friends. You're only allowed to run sideways, like a crab!

Fishy cat
In South East Asia there is a wild cat that goes fishing. The fishing cat is a good swimmer, and hunts for fish and other small animals in mangrove swamps.

What is a sea cow?

Sea cows aren't really cows. They are dugongs and manatees – huge, sausage-shaped sea creatures, a bit like seals. Like a real cow, sea cows graze on plants, such as sea grass and mangrove leaves.

where do turtles lay their eggs?

Sea turtles live in the sea, but lay their eggs on land. Female turtles crawl up sandy beaches at night, and dig holes with their flippers, in which they lay their eggs. Then they cover them over with sand, and leave them to hatch.

← Turtle

Why do baby turtles race to the sea?

When turtle eggs hatch, baby turtles climb out of their sandy nest and head for the sea. They must reach the water quickly, before they get gobbled up by a seabird, crab or fox.

Salty nose

The marine iguana is a lizard that swims in the sea. As it rests on rocks to warm up, salt from the sea makes a white patch on its nose.

Find out
There are different types of turtle. Look in books or on the Internet to find out what they are.

Which seabird has a colourful beak?

Puffins have bright beaks striped with orange, yellow and black. In spring, their beaks and feet become brighter, to help them find a mate. Males and females rub their beaks together to show they like each other.

Puffins

Quiz time

Do you remember what you have read about the seashore? Here are some questions to test your memory. The pictures will help you. If you get stuck, read the pages again.

3. Do beetles head for the beach?
page 171

4. Can you tell a pebble from an egg?
page 172

1. How long is the seashore?
page 164

5. Why are pebbles round?
page 175

page 167

2. How big are the biggest waves?

6. Are seashells different shapes?
page 177

7. How do penguins get out of the water? page 177

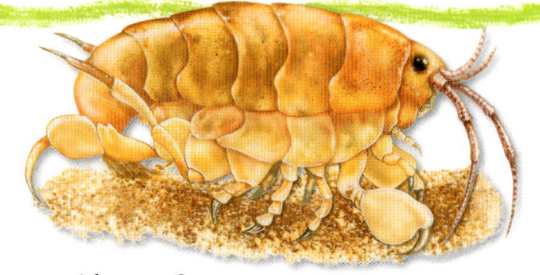

8. Why does glass come from the seashore? page 179

9. What hides in the sand? page 180

10. Which fish can walk on land? page 183

11. Are there fleas at the beach? page 185

12. What is a sea cow? page 187

13. Why do baby turtles race to the sea? page 189

Answers

1. Thousands of kilometres long
2. The biggest waves (tsunamis) can be 30 metres high
3. The tiger beetle does
4. You might not be able to, the ringed plover lays eggs that look like pebbles
5. Because they have been rolled and tumbled around by waves
6. Yes they are
7. They zoom up to the surface and shoot out of the water
8. Because it's made from sand
9. Worms, shrimps, razorshells and some crabs
10. The mudskipper
11. No, but there are sandhoppers
12. Dugongs and manatees
13. To avoid being gobbled up by predators

191

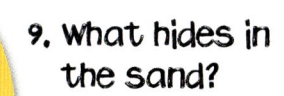

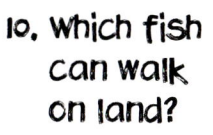

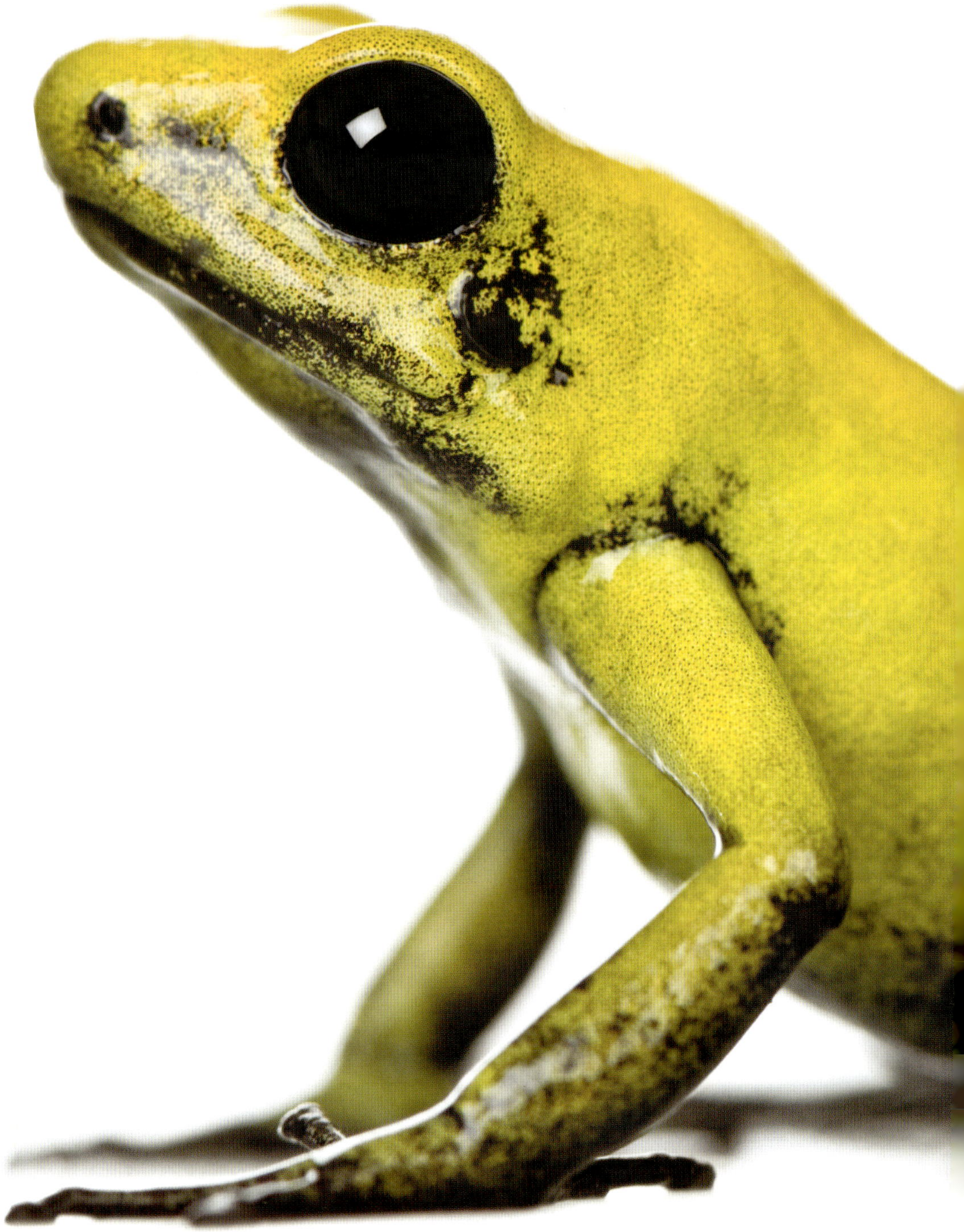

Rainforests

who lives in a rainforest?

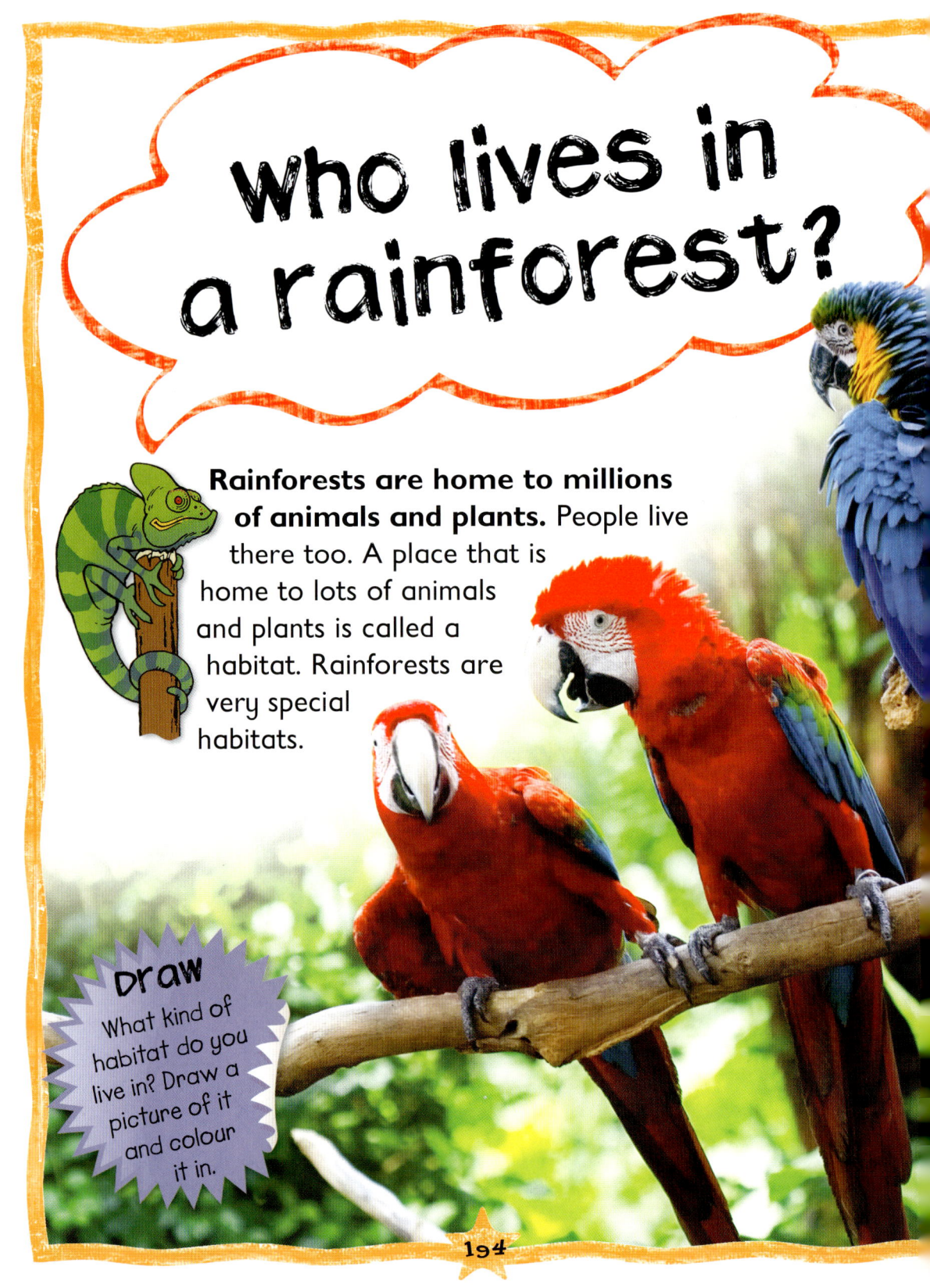

Rainforests are home to millions of animals and plants. People live there too. A place that is home to lots of animals and plants is called a habitat. Rainforests are very special habitats.

Draw
What kind of habitat do you live in? Draw a picture of it and colour it in.

Which lizard can bark?

There are not many dogs in the jungle, but there are lizards that bark! They are called tokay geckos. Their bark sounds like 'to-kay, to-kay'. These lizards climb trees and hunt bugs at night.

Macaws

Big mouth
Potoos are jungle birds that eat insects at night. They have big, gaping mouths and swallow their food whole.

Why do parrots talk?

Parrots talk for the same reason we do — they need to tell each other things. When most parrots talk they twitter, screech and squawk. Some sounds are a warning. They tell other parrots that danger may be nearby.

Why do toucans have big bills?

Toucans are birds with big, colourful bills (beaks). Both males and females have big bills, so they might be useful in attracting a mate. They may also help toucans reach and eat fruit high up in the trees.

Toucan

How big is a Goliath spider?

Goliath spiders are huge! They live in the rainforests of South America and can have a leg span of up to 30 centimetres. They eat insects and sometimes catch small birds to eat. Luckily, these spiders are harmless to people.

Goliath spider

Make
Use a paper plate, pipe cleaners and tape to make a life-size model of a Goliath spider.

Does it rain every day in a rainforest?

It rains almost every day in a rainforest. This habitat is home to plants that need lots of rain and plenty of hot, sunny days. Without rain and warmth, rainforest plants cannot grow.

Yum yum!
Leeches are slug-like animals that live in rainforest rivers. They love to suck blood from animals and humans!

How slow is a sloth?

Sloths are possibly the slowest animals alive. They are so slow, it is almost impossible to see one moving. Sloths hang upside down in trees. Once a week, they slowly climb to the ground to poo. It takes them one minute to walk 2 metres!

Baby sloth

Does chocolate grow on trees?

No, chocolate doesn't grow on trees, but the beans we use to make chocolate do. They are called cacao beans, and they grow in big pods on cacao trees.

Cacao pods

Scratch and sniff!
Tapirs use their long snouts to sniff for food. They scratch around in mud to find berries and fruit.

Why do monkeys howl?

Monkeys are very noisy animals. They live in groups, and need to howl, chatter and hoot to talk to one another. Howler monkeys live in South American jungles. They are some of the loudest animals in the world.

Go slow
Pretend to be a sloth. Measure 2 metres and see how slowly you can walk that distance.

Which jungle cat has spots?

Jaguars are spotty jungle cats. Spots and stripes help animals to hide. Jaguars live in jungles and hide in trees and bushes. When they see or hear an animal they jump out and attack. Using colours and patterns to blend in is called camouflage.

Jaguar

Hide
Wear clothes that are a similar colour or pattern to your surroundings. How well hidden are you?

Can lizards change colour?

Chameleons are lizards that can change colour. They may turn pink, red, green, blue, brown, yellow or even purple. Chameleons change colour when they are angry, or excited. They can also become the same colour as their surroundings.

Slime time!

Pitcher plants are bug-eating plants. Flies fall inside them, and get trapped in pools of liquid. The plants have slimy walls to stop flies escaping.

Rafflesia flower

Which flower smells of rotting meat?

Rafflesias plants have huge flowers up to 100 centimetres wide. These flowers have a very strong, nasty smell, like rotting meat, and this attracts insects to them.

Which beetle is a giant?

Most beetles are smaller than a fingernail, but one is longer than your hand. It is a Hercules beetle, and males can grow to 19 centimetres long. They have long horns on their heads, which they use to fight each other.

Hercules beetle

Agouti

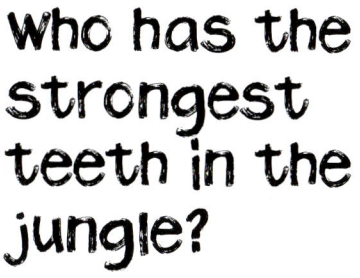

Who has the strongest teeth in the jungle?

Agoutis have such strong teeth they can bite through hard nut shells. Few animals are able to open the tough shells of Brazil nuts. Agoutis can bite through them to eat the tasty nut inside.

Big bird!
A cassowary is a bird, but it cannot fly. Cassowaries have sharp claws on their feet, and they kick out if they're scared by intruders.

Count
If an agouti eats five nuts every day, how many will it eat in two days?

Can a piranha eat a horse?

No, a single piranha can't eat a horse, but a group, or shoal, could. Piranhas are fierce fish that live in some rainforest rivers, and they have very sharp teeth. When a group of piranhas attack, they can eat a big animal in minutes.

Do kangaroos live in trees?

Kangaroos don't live in trees – unless they're tree kangaroos! The furry tree kangaroo is small enough to climb trees and walk along branches. It sleeps in the day and feeds on leaves and flowers at night.

Tree kangaroo

What is a bird of paradise?

Birds of paradise are some of the most beautiful birds in the world. The males have fine feathers in many colours. Some birds grow long tail feathers. They show off their feathers to females when it is time to mate.

King bird of paradise

Raggiana bird of paradise

Princess Stephana's bird of paradise

Good-looking!

Quetzals are colourful jungle birds. Males grow long tail feathers that can reach one metre in length!

Draw

Draw a bird of paradise and decorate it using pens, glue and scraps of brightly coloured paper.

How do lizards fly?

Lizards cannot really fly because they don't have wings, but some lizards can glide. They have flaps of skin that they stretch out to glide through the air when they leap from a tree.

205

What is the biggest butterfly?

Millions of butterflies and moths flutter through the world's rainforests. One of the biggest is Queen Alexandra's birdwing butterfly. It can measure nearly 30 centimetres from wing tip to wing tip.

Queen Alexandra's birdwing butterfly

why are jungle frogs so deadly?

Not all jungle frogs are deadly, but some have poisonous skin. Most poison-arrow frogs are small, and have colourful skin that is coated with poison. The golden poison-arrow frog is one of the deadliest of all, but it is no bigger than your thumb.

Golden poison-arrow frog

sweet bird!
Hummingbirds feed on the sweet juice made by flowers. When they hover at a flower, their wings make a humming sound.

who eats all the leaves?

The floor of the forest is covered with dead leaves. Some of them will rot away. Others will be eaten by the billions of tiny animals that live in a jungle – such as ants, caterpillars, slugs and snails.

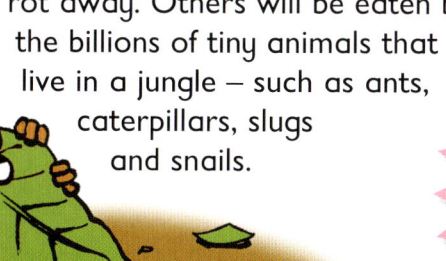

Find
Look under plants and stones to see garden animals, such as ants, beetles, and woodlice. Try not to disturb them.

Do lemurs wear rings on their tails?

No, lemurs do not wear rings on their tails! Ring-tailed lemurs have bands of black-and-white fur on their tails, which look like rings. When they walk, the lemurs wave their long furry tails in the air.

Ring-tailed lemur

Find out
Using the Internet, find out the name of the island that lemurs live on. What other animals live there?

Who is as thin as a pencil?

A baby vine snake is as thin as a pencil. An adult vine snake is about as thin as a grown-up's finger. Vine snakes live in trees and hunt birds and lizards to eat.

Vine snake

Bug cleaner!
Ring-tailed lemurs roll giant millipedes over their fur! It's thought that the millipedes release a chemical that keeps pesky flies and bugs off the lemurs.

Why don't bats bump into trees?

Most jungle bats fly at the night. They don't bump into trees because they have a special sense that helps them to work out where things are, even in the dark. It is called echolocation.

Are there dragons in the jungle?

There are no real dragons in the jungle, but there are lizards that look like dragons! Boyd's dragon is an iguana that has a flap of skin under its chin, called a dewlap. It also has a row of spines that run along its back.

Boyd's dragon

When is a leaf not a leaf?

When it is a leaf insect! Some rainforest insects pretend to be leaves or sticks. This means they can stay still and hide from birds and lizards that want to eat them. They also hide from other bugs they want to catch.

Leaf insect

Freeze
Lie on the floor like a leaf insect and stay still for as long as you can.

Yummy honey!
Sun bears have very strong claws for digging into bees' nests. They lick out the honey with their long tongues.

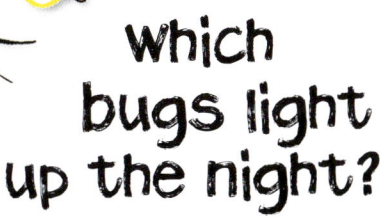

Which bugs light up the night?

Glow insects do. Some of these bugs are called glow-worms and others are called fireflies. Hundreds of them gather in a tree, and twinkle like Christmas lights, or stars in the sky.

Who lives in the clouds?

Gorillas live in cloud forests, where the tops of the trees are covered in mist and cloud. These rainforests are often wet and cool, but gorillas don't mind. They have thick fur, and spend most of the day eating leaves, playing and sleeping.

Baby gorilla

Red-eyed tree frogs

Which frog has scary eyes?

Red-eyed tree frogs use their big red eyes to scare enemies. If disturbed, the frogs flash their bulging eyes. This may startle predators and scare them away.

Find it
Use an atlas or the Internet to find the Amazon River in the Amazon rainforest. It's in South America.

Smashing chimps!
Clever chimps use stones as tools to crack open tough nuts and fruits.

Why do animals move home?

When part of a rainforest dies, or is cut down, the animals that live there move to find a new place to live. Every year, many animals lose their homes when people cut down trees in rainforests.

Why are tigers stripy?

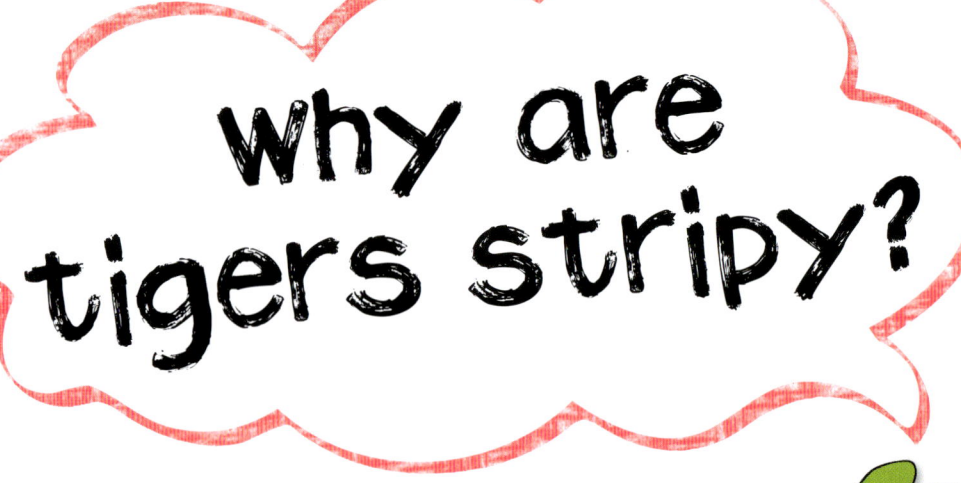

Stripes may help tigers to hide while they hunt. It is difficult to spot a striped animal hiding in the shadows. Tigers often crouch in long grass waiting for an animal to pass by. Then they pounce!

Tiger

can apes be orange?

Some apes are orange! Orang-utans are large apes that live in jungles in Asia. Their fur is long, and orange-brown. Baby orang-utans stay with their mothers until they are about 8 years old.

Mother and baby orang-utan

Think
Orang-utans are apes. Can you think of any other types of ape?

Do all birds live in trees?

Most birds live in trees, where they are safe from other animals. But some, such as the junglefowl, spend a lot of time on the ground. They find bugs, seeds and worms to eat there.

Giant frog!
Goliath frogs live in jungle rivers and lakes, and are big enough to swallow lizards. They can be more than 30 centimetres long!

Which bird is Lord of the Jungle?

The Philippine eagle is called the 'Lord of the Jungle'. It is one of the biggest birds in the world. This eagle has huge talons (claws) and a strong, curved bill. It hunts other birds, snakes, wild cats, lemurs and even monkeys.

Flying lemur

Philippine eagle

When is a toad like a leaf?

When it is hidden on the forest floor! Some jungle frogs and toads have colours and patterns that help them to hide on trees, leaves or branches. The leaflitter toad has brown camouflage that makes it look like a dead leaf.

Leaflitter toad

Tongue-twister!

Okapis have very long tongues. They are so long, an okapi can use its tongue to lick its eyeballs clean!

Why are some animals rare?

When the number of a species (type) of animal falls, it is said to be rare. Tigers, orang-utans and gorillas are rare. Animals become rare when they cannot find enough food, or their home in the wild has gone.

Think

Make up a story about three jungle animals and an adventure they have.

Why does a snake squeeze its food?

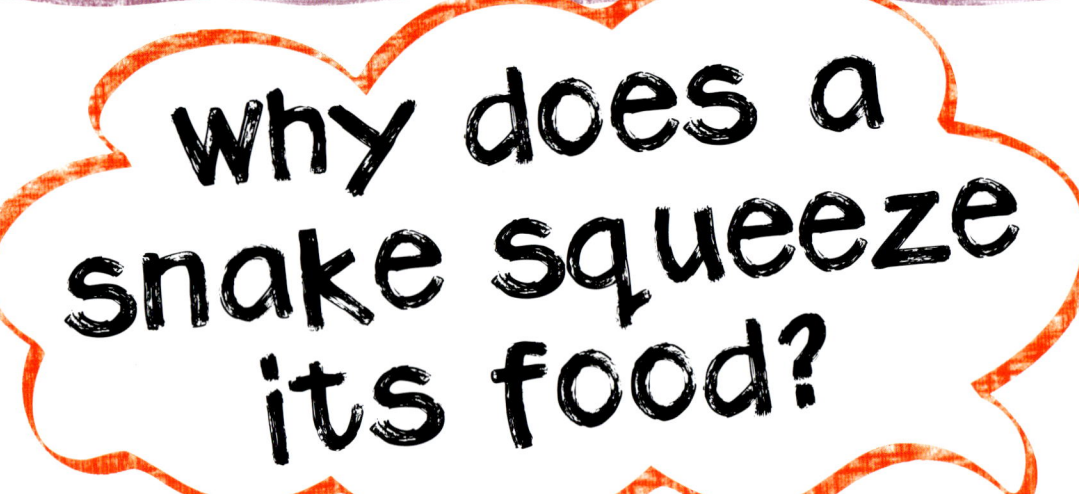

So it can eat it! The emerald tree boa is a rainforest snake. Once it has grabbed its prey, it wraps its body around it and squeezes it to death. This snake can grow to 2 metres long.

Emerald tree boa

Forest elephants

Who has the biggest teeth in the jungle?

Elephants have the biggest teeth, called tusks. African forest elephants have tusks that point down, so they can walk through plants and trees without getting their tusks tangled in leaves!

Record
It rains almost every day in rainforests. Make a chart to record the weather every day for one month.

Do monkeys have beards?

Mangabey monkeys have tufts of white hair that look like beards! These may help the monkeys to communicate. Mangabeys live in the Africa, in groups called 'troops'.

Sticky toes!
Gecko lizards are able to crawl on rocks and trees because they have sticky toes. Tiny hairs on their toes work like glue, to make them stick.

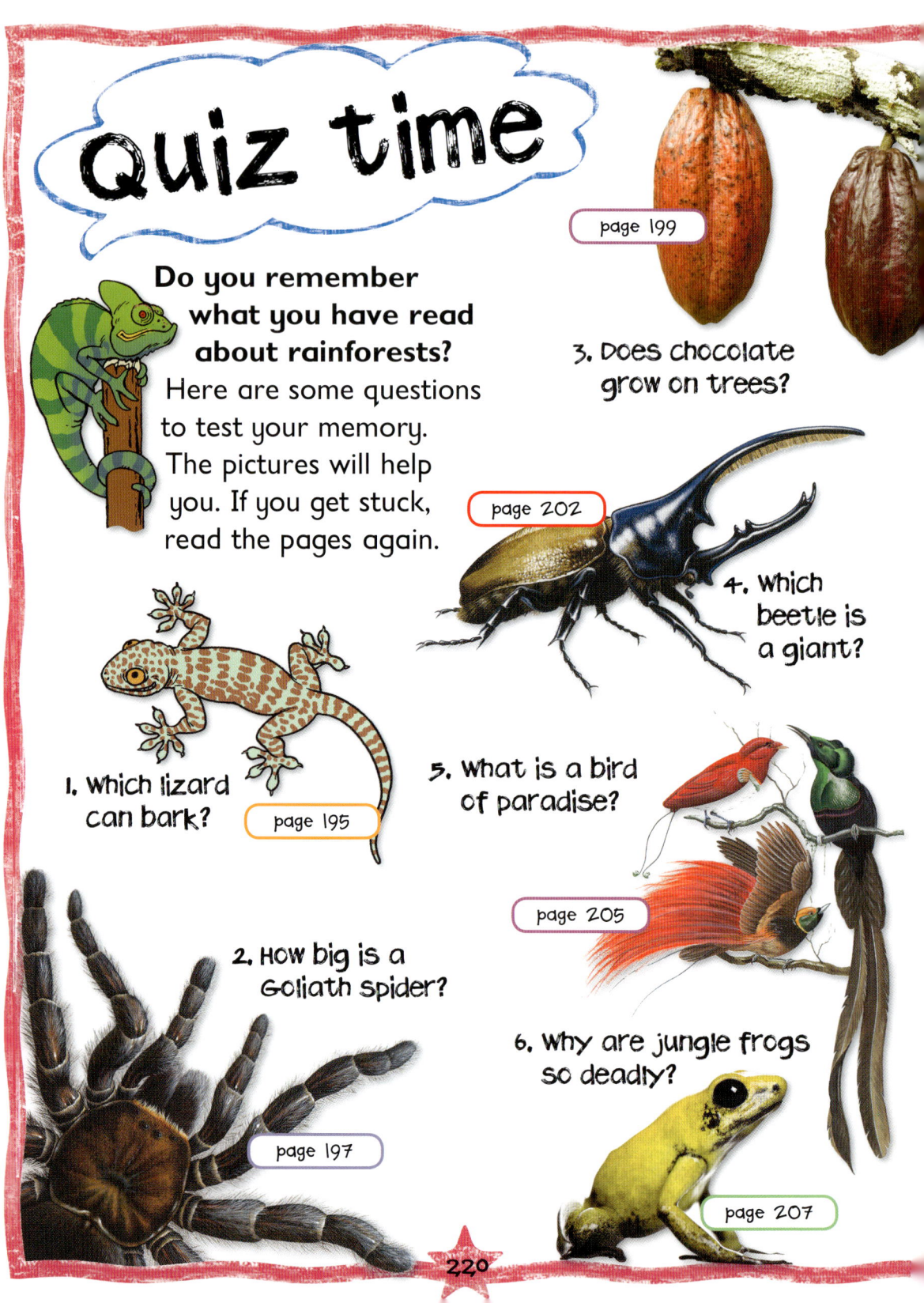

Quiz time

Do you remember what you have read about rainforests? Here are some questions to test your memory. The pictures will help you. If you get stuck, read the pages again.

page 199

3. Does chocolate grow on trees?

page 202

4. Which beetle is a giant?

1. Which lizard can bark?

page 195

5. What is a bird of paradise?

page 205

2. How big is a Goliath spider?

page 197

6. Why are jungle frogs so deadly?

page 207

page 209

7. Who is as thin as a pencil?

page 216

11. Which bird is Lord of the Jungle?

page 211

12. Why are some animals rare?

page 217

8. When is a leaf not a leaf?

page 218

9. Why do animals move home?

page 213

13. Why does a snake squeeze its food?

10. Do all birds live in trees?

page 215

Answers

1. The tokay gecko
2. They have a leg span of 30 centimetres
3. No, but cacao beans do, and these are used to make chocolate
4. The Hercules beetle
5. A beautiful bird with bright feathers and a long tail
6. Because some have poisonous skin
7. The vine snake
8. When it's a leaf insect
9. Because their rainforest homes are cut down
10. No, some spend a lot of time on the ground
11. The Phillipine eagle
12. Because they don't have enough food or their homes have disappeared
13. So it can eat it

221

222

Coral Reef

Is a coral reef alive?

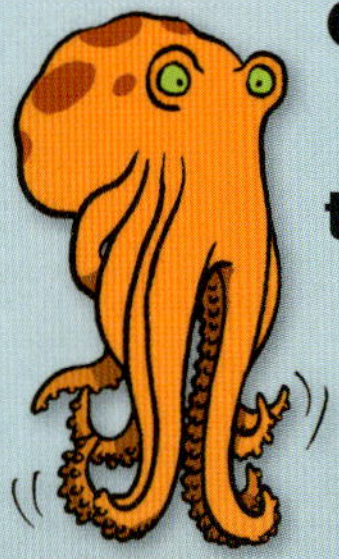

Coral reefs are living structures that grow in the sea. They are built by millions of tiny animals, called coral polyps. When they die, new polyps grow on top. This builds up layers of coral rock over time. Some reefs, such as the Great Barrier Reef, are enormous and can be seen from the air.

Great Barrier Reef

Coral

Do trees grow underwater?

Trees do not grow underwater, but soft tree corals look like trees because they have branches. Coral reefs are sometimes called 'rainforests of the sea'. Like rainforests on land, coral reefs are important homes for millions of marine animals.

Soft tree coral

Big brains
Octopuses are super smart animals that live near reefs. They are experts at finding prey hiding in rocky crevices.

Draw
Choose your favourite fish from this book. Draw it onto paper and colour it in.

How do coral polyps feed?

Coral polyps live in hard, stony cups and feed on tiny animals that drift by in the water. They catch food with tiny stingers on their tentacles, as do jellyfish, which are in the same animal family as coral polyps.

can turtles swim far?

Turtles go on very long journeys across the sea to feed, mate or lay their eggs. Female turtles always return to the same beach to lay their eggs. How they find their way is still a mystery, but they don't seem to get lost!

Discover
Use an atlas to find out which country beginning with 'A' is near the Great Barrier Reef.

Turtles from *Finding Nemo*

When does a fish look like a stone?

When it is a stonefish! These fish are almost impossible to see when they are lying flat and still on the seabed. Their colours blend in with the rocky and sandy surfaces.

Stonefish

Show-offs

Cuttlefish can change colour! In just a few seconds, a cuttlefish can flash colours of red, yellow, brown or black.

Do seahorses gallop?

Seahorses are fish, not horses, so they cannot run or gallop. They are not very good swimmers so they wrap their tails around seaweed to stop ocean currents carrying them away.

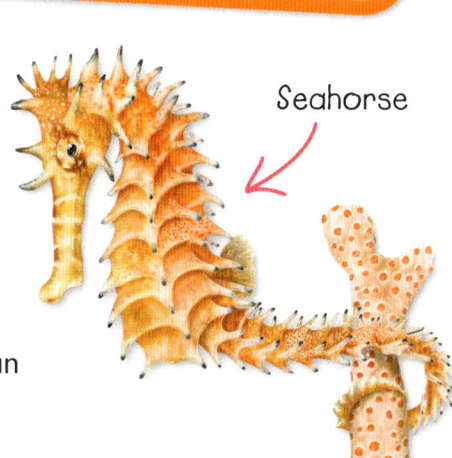

Seahorse

Why are fish like lions?

Lionfish

Some fish are like lions because they hunt for food at night. Lionfish hide among rocks in the day. As the sun sets, they come out to hunt for small animals to eat. They have amazing stripes and spines on their bodies. Their spines hold venom, which can cause very painful stings.

Dive and stay alive

Divers can use cages to watch sharks safely. The divers wear masks and carry tanks that have air inside them so they can breathe underwater.

when do birds visit reefs?

Birds visit coral reef islands to build their nests. When their eggs hatch, the birds find plenty of fish at the reef to feed to their chicks. Albatrosses are large sea birds, so their chicks need lots of fish!

count

If an albatross chick needs to eat two big fish every day, how many fish will it eat in five days?

can slugs be pretty?

Yes they can! Like many coral reef animals, sea slugs have amazing colours and patterns. These warn other animals that they are harmful to eat. Most sea slugs are small, but some can grow to 30 centimetres in length.

Sea slugs

What lives on a reef?

A huge number of different animals live on or around reefs. They are home to fish of all shapes and sizes, including sharks. There are many other animals too — octopus, squid, slugs, sponges, starfish and urchins all live on reefs.

Sea grasses   Black sea urchin   Sea turtle   Starfish

Which sea creature eats weeds?

Sea urchins help to keep the reef healthy by grazing on algae, seagrasses and seaweed. If there is too much seaweed on a reef, it can block the light, which the coral polyps need to grow.

A sting in the tail

Blue-spotted rays live in coral reefs and feed on shellfish, crabs and worms. They have stinging spines on their tails.

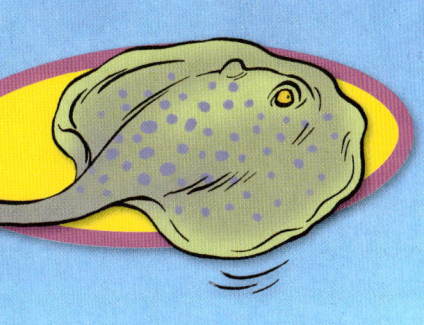

What do coral reefs need to grow?

The polyps that build up coral reefs need plenty of sunlight and clean water to grow. They mostly live in shallow water near land where sunlight can reach them.

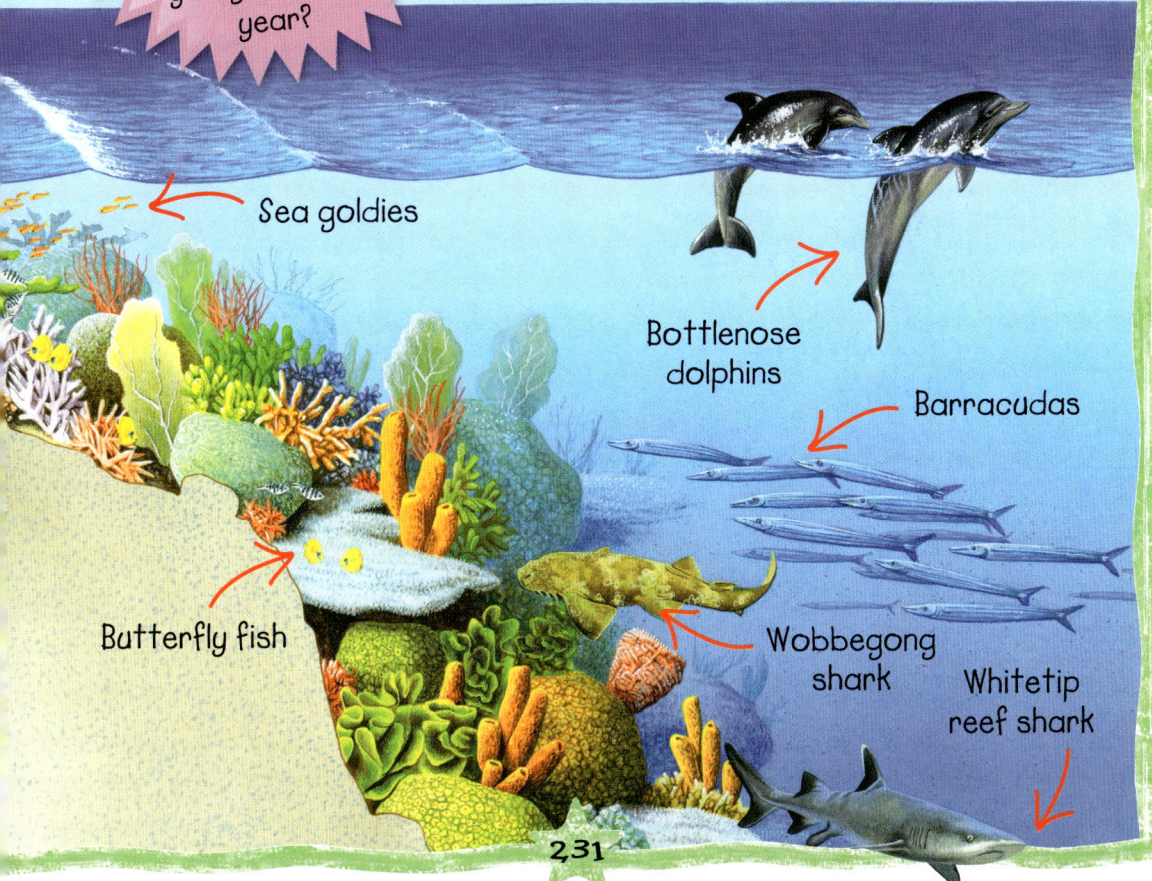

Measure

Every year coral reefs grow about 10 centimetres. How much have you grown in a year?

Sea goldies

Bottlenose dolphins

Barracudas

Butterfly fish

Wobbegong shark

Whitetip reef shark

can parrots swim?

Of course not – parrots are birds that live in jungles! Parrotfish, however, are dazzling, colourful fish that swim around reefs, nibbling at the coral. They have beak-like mouths, which is why they are named after parrots.

Parrotfish

Think
Make up a story about a leafy seadragon and a parrotfish. Draw pictures to tell your story.

Leafy seadragon

Which animal looks like seaweed?

A type of seahorse called a leafy seadragon does. Its strange shape makes it hard to spot when it swims around seaweed, hiding it from big fish that might want to eat it.

Do sponges help build reefs?

Sometimes — sponges are animals that bore, or dig, holes into coral. This can weaken a reef. However, when sponges die their bodies build up extra layers, which add to the reef structure.

Deadly jelly
Box jellyfish have deadly stings on their tentacles. Divers and swimmers stay away from them.

Why does an octopus have eight arms?

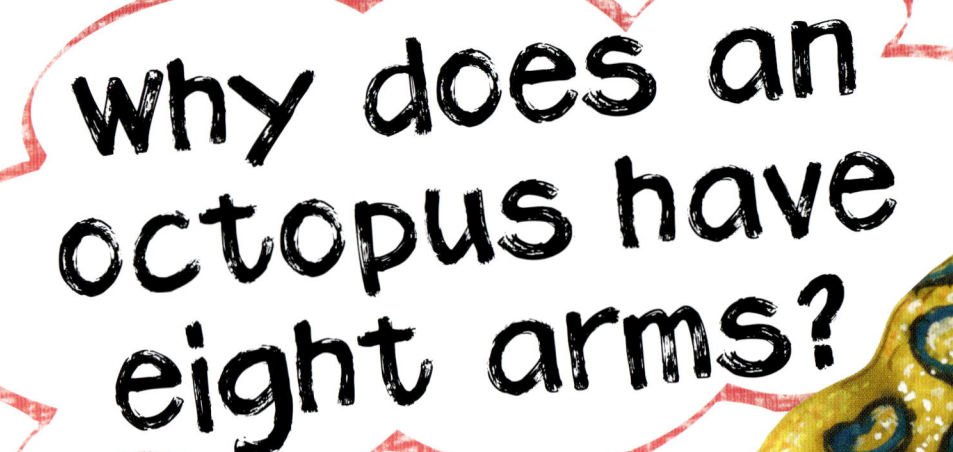

Having eight arms allows an octopus to move quickly and grab food to eat. Each arm has suction cups that can grip onto things. An octopus grabs food with its eight strong arms, and pulls it towards its mouth.

Make
Draw lots of pictures of coral reef animals and stick them on a large piece of card to make a poster.

Blue-ringed octopus

Who looks after a seahorse's eggs?

Females lay the eggs, but the males look after them in a special pouch on the front of their bodies. This keeps the eggs safe from bigger fish that might eat them. When the eggs hatch, the babies swim out of the pouch.

Don't eat me!
Little coral polyps live next to each other, but they do not always get on. Sometimes one polyp might eat its neighbour!

Do Christmas trees grow on reefs?

Christmas trees do not grow on reefs – but Christmas tree worms do. These little animals live in burrows inside the reef. The feathery, spiral parts we can see are called feeding tentacles.

Christmas tree worm

where do clownfish live?

Clownfish live in the tentacles of coral reef creatures called sea anemones. Like coral polyps, these strange-looking animals sting their prey. Clownfish have a slimy skin covering that protects them from the sting and allows them to live there unharmed.

Sea anemone

Hide
Invite some friends to join you in a game of hide and seek. Where could you hide?

Clownfish

Shark attack

Some coral sharks aren't aggressive and people can feed them by hand. Bull sharks aren't so relaxed and have been know to attack divers.

Which fish flies around the reef?

The manta ray does. Its huge triangle-shaped fins are flapped like wings to move the ray through the water. Some manta rays can be up to 5 metres wide.

Manta Ray

Which shrimp likes to punch its prey?

Mantis shrimps may be small, but they can pack a big punch. They live in reefs near Australia and in the Pacific Ocean. They punch their prey to stun it, and then tuck in to a tasty meal.

can starfish be blue?

Most starfish are red or brown, but big blue ones live on some reefs. Starfish have small, tube-like feet on the undersides of their arms, which allow them to crawl over the reef. They have tiny eyes at the end of each arm, which can only see light or dark.

Starfish

Make
Make a map that shows where pirate treasure is buried on a coral island.

Do jellyfish wobble?

No, jellyfish may look like jelly, but they are living animals. They have long, stinging tentacles that hang below their bodies as they swim. Some jellyfish live around coral reefs, where there are plenty of fish to eat.

Box jellyfish

Fish hotspot

There are more than 24,000 different types of fish in the world. Many of those live in or around coral reefs.

Why did pirates bury treasure on coral islands?

Pirates are believed to have buried stolen treasure so no one could find it. There are lots of stories about pirates who buried gold and precious stones on coral islands, but we don't know how true these tales are.

Why are corals different shapes?

The shape a coral grows into depends on the type of polyp it has. Where the coral grows on the reef is also important. Brain coral grows slowly and in calm water. Staghorn and elkhorn corals grow more quickly, and in shallow water.

Brain coral

Elkhorn coral

Staghorn coral

Are there butterflies in the sea?

There is a type of butterfly living in the sea — but it isn't an insect, it's a fish! Many butterfly fish have colourful spots and stripes to help make them hard to spot.

Butterfly fish

LOOK
Find out if you can see colours better in the dark or in the light.

Going for a spin
Dolphins visit coral reefs to feast on fish. They jump out of the water and can even spin, though no one knows why they do it.

Can fish see in the dark?

Many animals can see in the dark. Lots of coral animals sleep during the day, but at night they come out to look for food or mates. Many, such as the red soldierfish, are much better at seeing in the dark than people are.

Which crab moves house?

Hermit crabs live inside borrowed shells and move house if they find a bigger, better one. They don't have their own shells so they have to find one to protect their soft bodies. Most hermit crabs choose snail shells to live in.

Hermit crab

Why is some coral white?

Most coral is very colourful, until it dies and turns white or grey. There are many reasons why corals are dying. Dirty water is one of the most important reasons. Water that is too warm is also bad for coral.

Damaged coral

Slow-growers
Giant clams can grow to be enormous – up to 150 centimetres long! They can live for 70 years.

Who looks after coral reefs?

Special ocean parks are set up to look after the animals that live on coral reefs. People are not allowed to catch the fish or damage the reef inside these protected areas.

Measure
Use a measuring tape to find out how long a giant clam is.

Why do coral fish dance?

To attract the attention of fish who might need a clean! Bluestreak cleaner wrasses feed on the parasites that attach themselves to the bodies of fish. When the wrasses are hungry, they dance around bigger fish, like moray eels, to let them know they are ready to clean.

Moray eel

Whale shark

Are all sharks dangerous?

No, most sharks would never attack a person. Whale sharks are huge but they don't eat big animals. They swim through the water with their large mouths open. They suck in water and any little creatures swimming in it.

Which crab wears boxing gloves?

Boxer crabs hold sea anemones in their claws, like boxing gloves. They wave them at any animals that come too close — the sight of the stinging tentacles warns other animals to stay away.

Wrasse

Brush
We don't have wrasses, so when you brush your teeth try hard to remove every tiny bit of food.

Special colours

Coral fish come in amazing colours and patterns. Good looks are important for survival. Blue and yellow fish look bright to us, but they are hidden on the reef by the way the sunlight is reflected.

245

Do sharks use hammers?

No, but some sharks have heads that look like hammers! These strange-looking sharks have wide, flattened heads. The shape might help them to find food, swim fast or change direction easily.

Hammerhead shark

Do squid change colour?

Yes, squid and octopuses are able to change colour, so they can hide, or send messages to each other. They can change colour very quickly – in just one or two seconds.

Caribbean reef squid

World wonder

No one had studied the Great Barrier Reef or the wildlife that lived on it until British explorer James Cook (1728–1779) sailed his ship right onto the reef, in 1770.

Which fish are shocking?

Electric rays can shock other animals by making electric charges in their bodies. As they swim over other fish, they stun them with powerful jolts of electricity. The rays then eat their prey whole, head first!

Dress

We change the way we look with the clothes we wear. How quickly can you change clothes?

247

which fish is spiky?

Pufferfish are strange-looking, poisonous fish with sharp spines. When they feel scared, pufferfish blow up their bodies to make their spines stand on end. This makes them bigger and much harder to swallow.

Pufferfish with spines relaxed

Pufferfish with spines on end

March
Imagine you are a lobster on a long march. How far can you march before you get tired?

Why do lobsters march?

Coral reef spiny lobsters march to deep, dark water where they lay their eggs. They march through the night at the end of the summer. Thousands of lobsters join the march to reach a safe place to breed.

Clean teeth
When fish such as sweetlips want their teeth cleaned, they swim to find wrasse fish and open their mouths.

Crown-of-thorns starfish

How do starfish eat their prey?

Starfish turn their mouths inside out to eat. The crown-of-thorns starfish kills coral by eating the soft polyps inside. Each of these large starfish can have up to 21 arms.

Quiz time

Do you remember what you have read about coral reefs? Here are some questions to test your memory. The pictures will help you. If you get stuck, read the pages again.

3. Why are fish like lions?

page 228

4. Which sea creature eats weeds?

page 230

5. Which animal looks like seaweed?

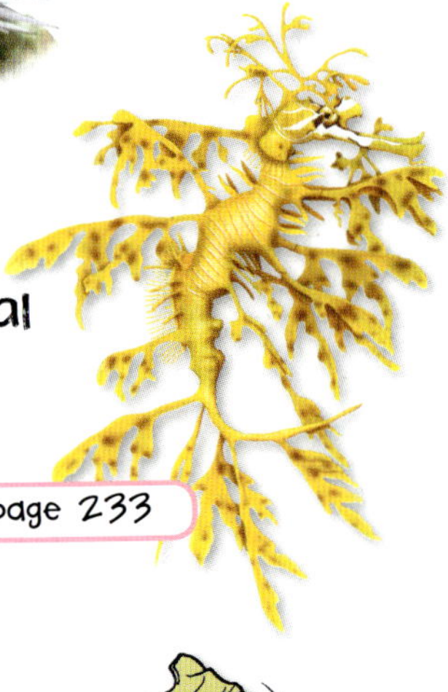

page 233

1. Do trees grow underwater?

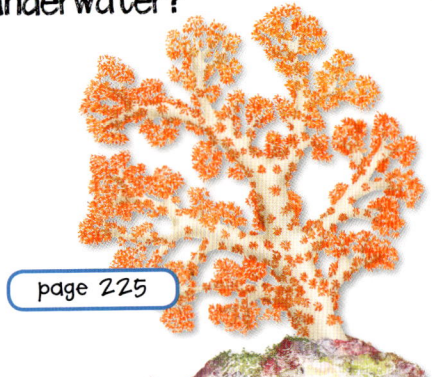

page 225

6. Who looks after a seahorse's eggs?

page 235

page 227

2. When does a fish look like a stone?

250

7. Where do clownfish live?
page 236

8. Do jellyfish wobble?
page 239

9. Can fish see in the dark?
page 241

10. Who looks after coral reefs?
page 243

11. Which crab wears boxing gloves?
page 245

12. Which fish are shocking?
page 247

13. Why do lobsters march?
page 249

Answers
1. No, but some corals have branches like trees
2. When it is a stonefish
3. Because they are hunters and come out to feed at night
4. Sea urchins eat seaweed
5. The leafy sea dragon
6. The male seahorse
7. In the tentacles of sea anemones
8. No, they are living animals and aren't made from jelly
9. Yes – many such as the red soldierfish can see well in the dark
10. Special ocean parks
11. The boxer crab
12. Electric rays
13. They march to an area where they can breed or lay their eggs

251

252

Big Cats

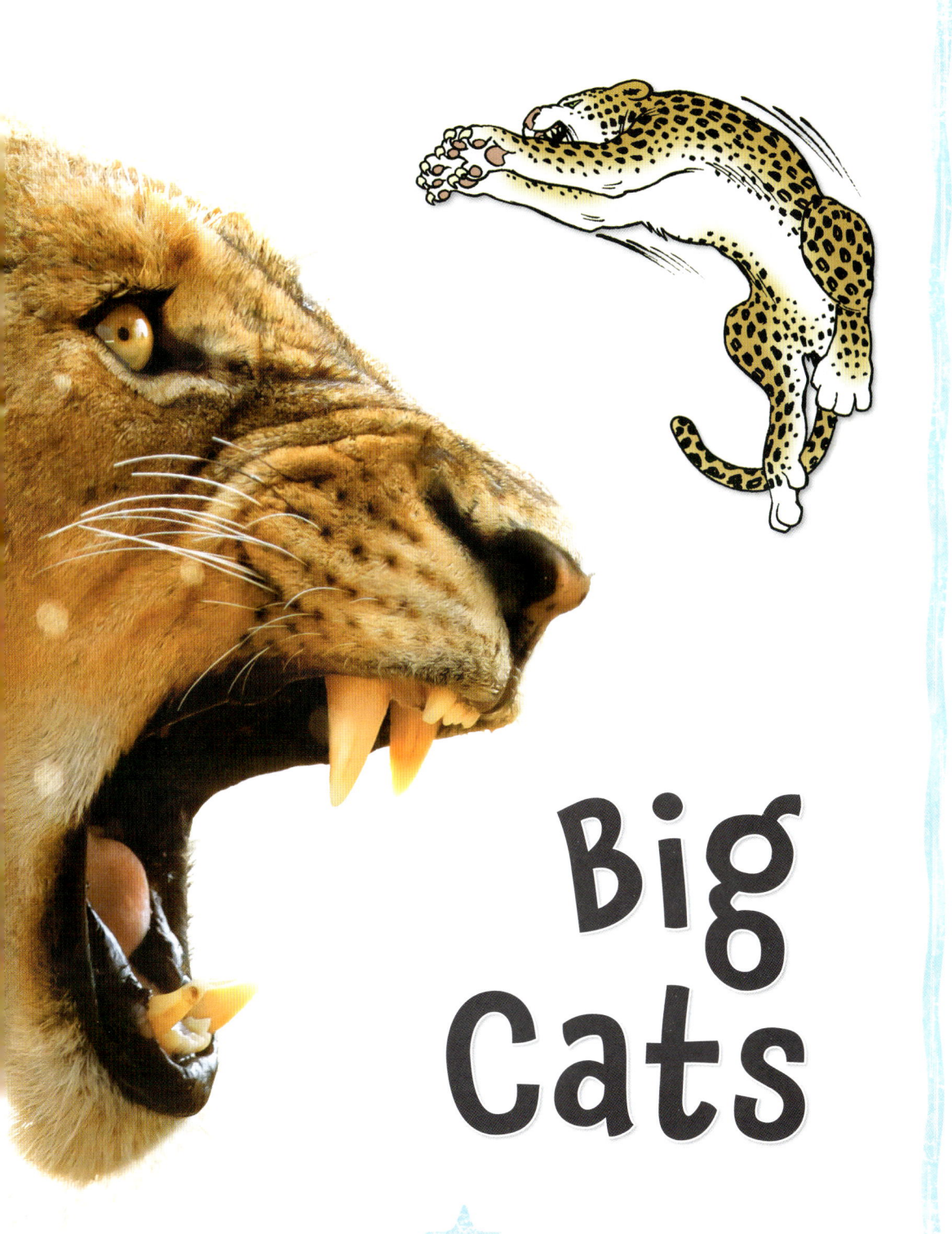

What is the biggest cat?

The Siberian tiger is the biggest cat, and one of the largest meat-eating animals in the world. The heaviest Siberian tiger was recorded at weighing 465 kilograms – that's the same weight as 23 of you! It also has thick fur to help it survive in freezing conditions.

Where do tigers live?

Tigers only live in southern and eastern Asia, in forests, woodlands and swamps. They used to live in much larger areas, but humans have now built houses and farms on much of the land. Siberian tigers live in snow-covered forests where temperatures can be −50°C.

Siberian tiger

Hair-head!
Male lion cubs begin to grow thick fur around their head and neck at about three years old. This fur is called a mane.

Why do lion cubs have to leave home?

Male lion cubs don't get to stay with their family group or pride, they get pushed out at about three years old. By then they are old enough to look after themselves. Soon they will take over new prides and have their own cubs.

Discover
Tigers are only found in certain parts of the world. Look on a map and see if you can find them.

What is a caracal?

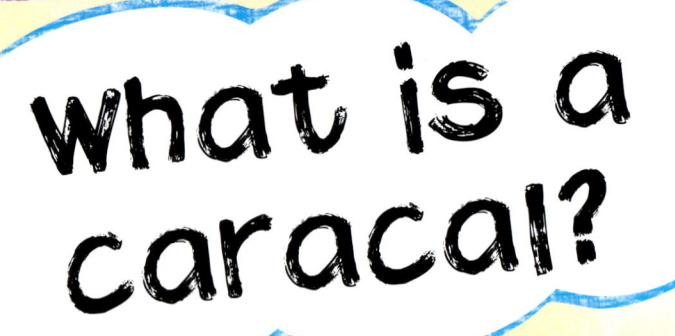

A caracal is a smaller type of wild cat that lives in hot, dry desert-like places. It hunts small animals, such as rats and hares, and can leap up to 3 metres high to catch a passing bird.

Caracal

Jaguar

Are jaguars good swimmers?

Jaguars are very good swimmers. Of all cats, they are the most water-loving. They like to live in swampy areas or places that flood during the rainy season, and they enjoy cooling off in rivers. Jaguars are mainly found in Central and South America.

Think
Jaguars are good swimmers. Can you think of some other animals that can swim?

Tiny kitty!
The black-footed cat of southern Africa is one of the smallest cats in the world. It's half the size of many pet cats.

Why do tiger cubs have to hide?

Tiger cubs hide behind their mothers for safety. Adult male tigers will kill any cubs that aren't their own. Less than half of the tiger cubs born in the wild live to the age of two years old.

Do big cats live in groups?

Lions are the only big cats that live in large family groups, called 'prides'. A pride is normally made up of four to six female lions, one or two males and their cubs. Some prides may have up to 30 animals if there is plenty of food nearby.

Pride of lions

Pretend

Imagine you are a prowling lion creeping up on your prey. See how slowly and quietly you can move.

Which cats can scream?

Small cats such as pumas make an ear-piercing scream instead of a roar. The cat family can be divided into two groups – big cats that can roar, and small cats that can't. A screaming cat can still be just as frightening!

Lady-lion hunt!

Female lions, called lionesses, do nearly all of the hunting for the pride. Male lions will only help with the hunt if it's a big animal such as a buffalo or a giraffe.

Why are lions lazy?

Lions seem lazy, but they have to rest to keep cool in the hot African sun. Usually, lions rest for around 20 hours a day. They normally hunt in the morning or at night when it's coolest. After a big meal they don't need to eat again for several days.

Are tigers always orange?

Most tigers are orange but a very small number are born white. All tigers have stripes. These help them to blend into their shadowy, leafy surroundings, making hunting easier. White tigers born in the wild are less likely to live as long as orange tigers because they do not blend in as well.

Tiger cubs

Lynx

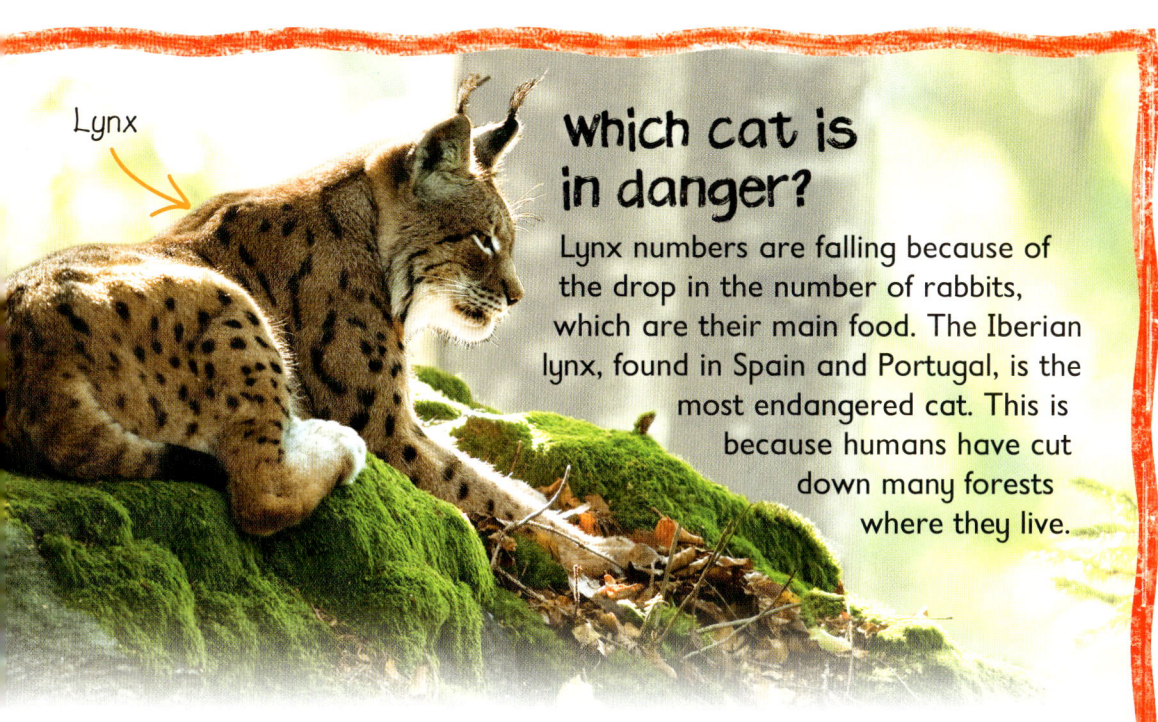

Which cat is in danger?

Lynx numbers are falling because of the drop in the number of rabbits, which are their main food. The Iberian lynx, found in Spain and Portugal, is the most endangered cat. This is because humans have cut down many forests where they live.

What do ocelots eat?

Ocelots, also called 'painted leopards', are small wild cats found mainly in South and Central America. They eat lots of different foods including rats, birds, frogs, monkeys, fish, tortoises and deer.

Think
How many types of food do you eat in a day? Is it as many as an ocelot?

Going, gone!
It's too late for some big cats. The Taiwan clouded leopard, and the Caspian, Bali and Javan tigers are extinct (have died out).

What is the bounciest cat?

The bounciest cat is the African serval. It can leap one metre high and travel 4 metres as it jumps. Unusually, it hunts in the day, for frogs, locusts and voles. Servals are like cheetahs, with slim, graceful, spotty bodies.

Serval

Do cats change their coats?

The lynx changes its coat with the weather. It lives in forests in northern Europe and Asia. In summer, the lynx's coat is short and light brown, but in winter its coat is much thicker, and light grey. This helps it to hide throughout the year.

Paw prints!
The stripes on a tiger are a bit like our fingerprints – no two animals have exactly the same pattern on their coats.

Why does a lion roar?

Lions roar to scare off other lions that stray onto their patch of land or territory. They also roar to let other members of their pride know where they are. A lion's roar is so loud it can be heard up to 10 kilometres away!

Roaring lion

Wear
Cats are kept warm by their thick coats of fur. Put on some furry clothes. Do they keep you warm?

Why do leopards climb trees?

Leopards climb trees to rest or to eat their food in safety. These big cats often kill prey that is larger than themselves. They are excellent climbers and are strong enough to drag their prey up into a tree, away from other hungry animals.

Leopard

Paint
Using face paints, ask an adult to make your face spotty like a leopard's.

How can humans help big cats?
Humans can help big cats by protecting areas of rainforest and grassland where they live. These areas are called 'reserves'. In a reserve, trees are not allowed to be cut down and the animals can live in safety.

Puma

No boat? Float!
Ancient Chinese soldiers used blown-up animal skins to cross deep rivers. They used their mouths to blow in air, then covered them with grease to keep it in.

What is a puma's favourite food?
Rabbits, hares and rats are favourite foods for a puma. They will attack bigger animals too. In places where humans have built their homes near the puma's natural surroundings, people have been attacked by these cats.

Can cheetahs run fast?

Yes they can – cheetahs are the world's fastest land animal. In a few seconds of starting a chase, a cheetah can reach its top speed of 105 kilometres an hour – as fast as a car! Cheetahs have 30 seconds to catch their prey before they run out of energy.

Why do people hunt big cats?

Mainly for their beautiful fur. For many years, cats have been killed in their hundreds of thousands so that people can wear their skins. Tigers especially were hunted for their body parts, which were used in Chinese medicines.

Make

With a paper plate and some straws for whiskers, make a tiger mask. Cut out eyeholes and paint it stripy!

Can't catch me!

Even though cheetahs are super-fast runners, only half of their chases end with a catch. Sometimes they scare their prey off before they get close enough to pounce.

Cheetah

Tiger

What time do tigers go hunting?

Almost all cats, including tigers, hunt at night. It is easier for a tiger to creep up on its prey when there is less light. A tiger may travel many kilometres each night while hunting. Tigers hunt deer, wild pigs, cattle and monkeys.

where do cheetahs live?

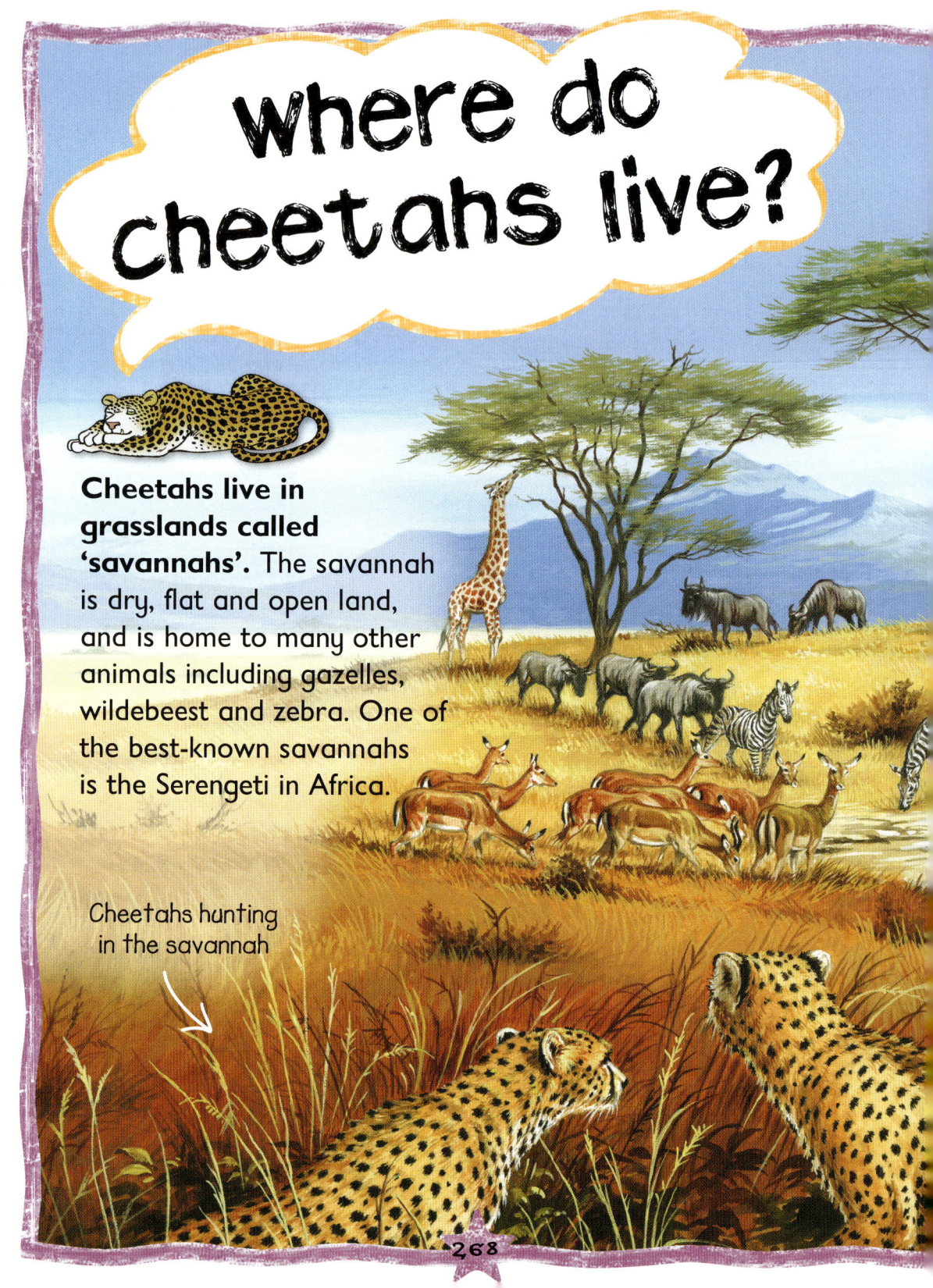

Cheetahs live in grasslands called 'savannahs'. The savannah is dry, flat and open land, and is home to many other animals including gazelles, wildebeest and zebra. One of the best-known savannahs is the Serengeti in Africa.

Cheetahs hunting in the savannah

Why do cats wash their faces?

Cats wash their faces to spread their scent over their body. Cats have scent-producing body parts called glands on their chin. They use their paws to wipe the scent from their glands and when the cat walks, it can mark its area, or territory.

Lion

Play
With a friend, collect some pebbles and sticks and use them to mark out your own territories in your garden.

Slow down!
In the wild, cheetahs have a short lifespan. Their running speed gets a lot slower as they get older so they are less successful when they hunt.

How often do tigers eat?

Sometimes, tigers don't even eat once a week. When tigers catch an animal they can eat 40 kilograms of meat. They don't need to eat again for eight or nine days.

What is a group of cubs called?

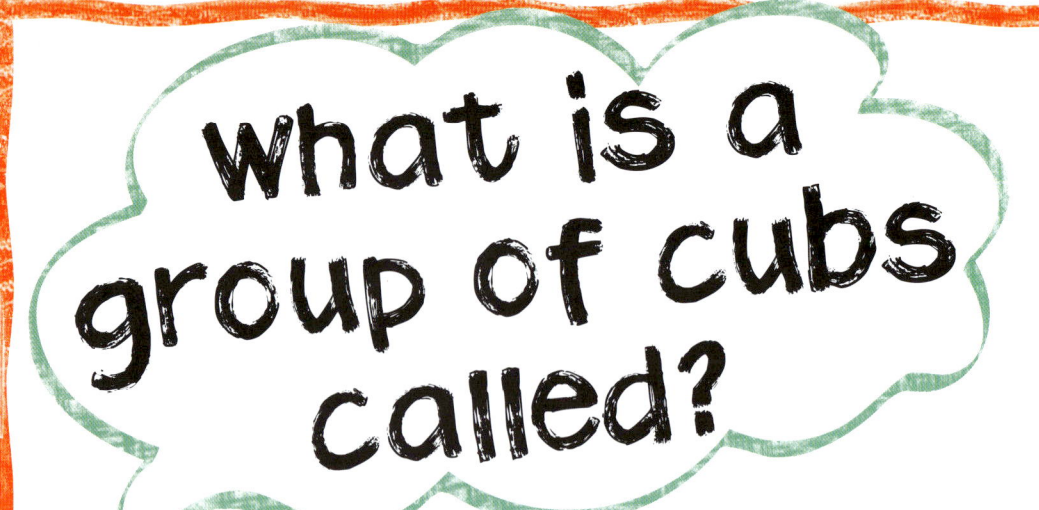

A group of cubs is called a litter. There are usually between two and four cubs in every litter. Cubs need their mother's milk for the first few months, but gradually they start to eat meat. The young of some cats, such as the puma, are called kittens.

Mother puma and litter of kittens

Sharpen your claws!

Unlike other cats, a cheetah's claws don't go back into its paws. This is why they don't often climb trees – they find it hard to get back down.

Leopards fighting

Why do leopards fight each other?

Leopards fight each other to defend their territory. Each leopard has its own patch of land, which it lives in. Leopards use scent-marking and make scratches on certain trees to warn other cats away.

Draw

Many different animals live in trees. Draw some pictures of animals that live in trees near you.

Which cat lives in the treetops?

Clouded leopards are excellent climbers and spend much of their time in the treetops of their forest home. These animals have been seen hanging upside-down from branches only by their back legs. Clouded leopards are brilliant swimmers, too.

Which big cats live in rainforests?

Tigers and leopards live in rainforests in India, and jaguars live in South American rainforests. Here, the weather stays hot all year, although there is often lots of rain.

Jaguar

What animals do jaguars hunt?

Young jaguars climb trees to hunt for birds and small animals. Adults are too heavy for the branches and hunt on the ground for deer, small mammals and sometimes cattle and horses.

Think
Are you as playful as the lion cubs? Invent some new games of your own to play with your friends.

Lion cubs

How do cubs learn to hunt?

Cubs learn to hunt by playing. Even a tortoise is a fun toy and by playing like this, cubs learn hunting skills. Many mothers bring their cubs a small, live animal so they can practice catching it.

It's a wrap!
The ancient Egyptians are well known for their 'mummies'. They even mummified animals including cats, birds and crocodiles.

How do snow leopards keep warm?

Snow leopard

Snow leopards live on snowy mountains in Central Asia. To keep warm in winter they grow a thick coat of fur and store extra layers of fat under their skin. They also wrap their long tails around their bodies when they sleep to keep in heat.

Which cat goes fishing?

The jaguar is an expert at fishing. Sometimes it waves its tail over the water to trick hungry fish before it strikes. Jaguars also fish for turtles and tortoises. Their jaws are so powerful that they can easily crack open a turtle shell.

Jaguar

Snowshoes!

Siberian tigers have large padded paws. They act as snowshoes and stop the tiger from sinking into the snow as it walks.

Make

Paint a picture of your favourite big cat. Make it as colourful as you like and give your big cat a name.

How do tigers stay cool?

Tigers such as the Bengal tiger live in places where it gets extremely hot in the summer. They can often be seen lying in pools of water to cool off, or resting in a shady area out of the hot sun.

Which cat is the most mysterious?

The clouded leopard is the most mysterious cat. It is so shy and rare that it is unusual to spot one. Clouded leopards grow to 2 metres in length, half of which is its tail. It uses its tail to balance as it leaps through the trees.

Clouded leopard

Why do cats always land on their feet?

Cats have bendy bodies and strong muscles. If a cat, such as a caracal, falls from a tree it can twist its body round so that it can land on its feet. Its muscles and joints take in the shock of the ground for a soft landing.

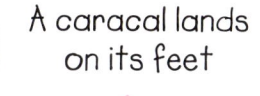

A caracal lands on its feet

Big teeth!
The sabre-toothed cat really did exist, about 10,000 years ago. It was the size of a small lion and its teeth were 25 centimetres long!

How many babies do tigers have?

Tigers normally have between two and four babies called cubs. The mother tiger is pregnant for three months, and the cubs are born blind. Most births happen at night, probably because it is safer.

Measure
Using a measuring tape, see if you can measure how long a clouded leopard is.

277

Why are cats the perfect hunters?

Because they have excellent eyesight and hearing, strong bodies and sharp teeth and claws. Many cats, such as lions, have fur that blends into their surroundings, which means they can hunt while staying hidden.

Lion hunting

How do cats see in the dark?

Cats have special cells at the back of their eyes that reflect light. They are able to see objects clearly even in dim light, which is why many cats hunt at night. Cats can see four times better in the dark than humans can.

Lioness at night

'Eye' can see you!

Cats have very good eyesight, in daylight and at night. For cats that live in grasslands, this helps them to spot distant prey on the open land.

Try

How well can you see in the dark? Turn off the light and wait for your eyes to adjust. Can you see anything?

Do big cats have enemies?

Big cats don't have many natural enemies. However, they watch out for animals, such as hyenas, that will gang up to steal their meal. A group of hyenas will attack and kill a big cat if it is weak or injured.

Quiz time

Do you remember what you have read about big cats? These questions will test your memory. The pictures will help you. If you get stuck, read the pages again.

page 261

3. Which cat is in danger?

4. What do ocelots eat?

page 261

page 254

1. What is the biggest cat?

page 262

5. What is the bounciest cat?

page 257

page 265

2. Are jaguars good swimmers?

6. How can humans help big cats?

7. Why do people hunt big cats?

page 266

8. What time do tigers go hunting?

page 267

9. Why do cats wash their faces?

page 269

10. Why do leopards fight each other?

page 271

11. Which cat is the most mysterious?

page 276

12. How many babies do tigers have?

page 277

13. Do big cats have enemies?

page 279

Answers

1. The Siberian tiger
2. Yes, they are
3. The lynx – especially the Iberian lynx
4. Rats, birds, frogs, monkeys, fish, tortoises and deer
5. The African serval
6. By creating protected reserves
7. For their fur
8. At night
9. To spread scent over their bodies
10. To defend their territories
11. The clouded leopard
12. Between two and four babies, or cubs
13. No, but hyenas can be a threat

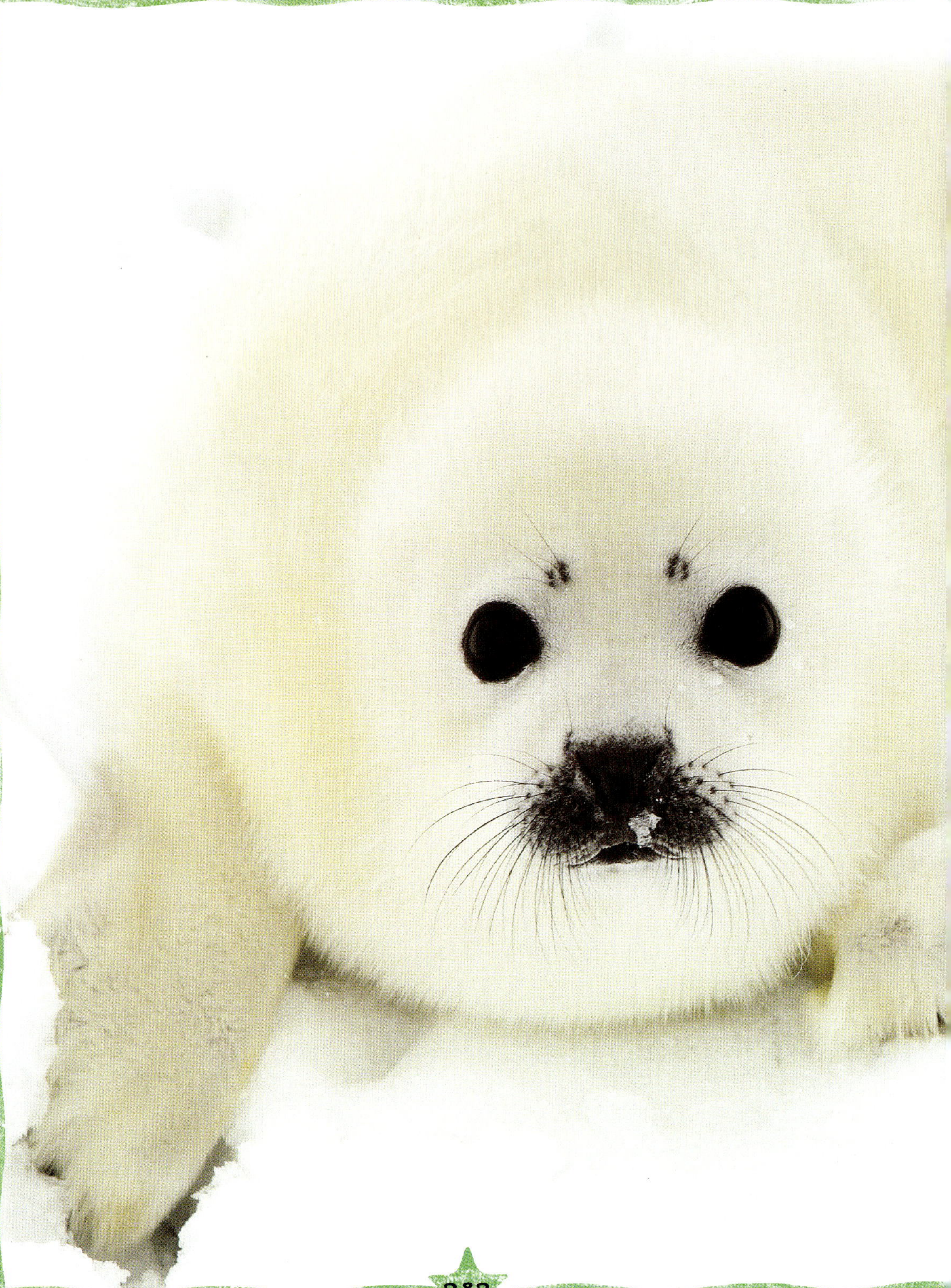

Baby Animals

Which baby has the best mum?

Many animals take great care of their young, but the orang-utan is one of the most caring. They feed their babies for at least three years and cuddle up close every night. A young orang-utan stays with its mum until it is about eight years old.

Baby orang-utan

Big eater!
A baby blue whale drinks nearly 400 litres of its mother's milk every day. That's about five bathfuls!

Which frog is the best dad?

The green poison-dart frog is! The male guards his eggs while they develop. Then, after the eggs have hatched into tadpoles, he takes them to a safe pool of water to grow.

Tadpoles

Green poison-dart frog

Find
What did you look like as a baby? Find some photos of you when you were a few months old.

What do baby frogs look like?

Baby frogs, called tadpoles, look very different from their parents. They are little swimming creatures with a tail and no legs. They have gills for breathing in water. As they get bigger, tadpoles grow legs and lose their tail.

Why do fawns have spots?

The spotty coat of a fawn (baby deer) makes it hard to see in its forest home. This is because the sun shines through leaves and twigs, making light spots on the forest floor – just like the spots on the fawn's coat.

Imagine
Pretend you are a mother bird and make a soft nest using blankets and pillows.

Fawn

How do monkeys clean their babies?

Monkeys groom their young with their fingers and pick out bits of dead skin, insects and dirt. Many animals also lick their babies to keep them clean.

Trunk call

Elephants use their trunks for many things, such as grabbing food from trees. Baby elephants have to learn to control their trunks.

Macaque monkey family

What do baby sharks eat?

Some eat other baby sharks! The eggs of the sand tiger shark hatch inside the mother's body. The first young to hatch then feed on the other eggs. When the sharks are born they are about one metre long.

Why do kangaroos have pouches?

Kangaroos have pouches to keep their babies safe. A baby kangaroo is called a joey and it is very weak and tiny when it is born. It lives in its mum's pouch where it feeds and grows until it is strong enough to look after itself.

Joey

Think
Puppy, kitten, chick... how many other names for baby animals can you think of?

Are turtles born in the sea?

Turtles live in the sea but lay their eggs on land. The mother turtle crawls up onto the beach and digs a pit in which to lay her eggs. When the eggs hatch, the babies make their way down to the sea.

Baby loggerhead turtle

Which animal has the longest pregnancy?

Pregnancy is the word used for the time it takes for a baby to grow inside its mother. The female elephant has the longest pregnancy of any animal – up to 21 months – that's nearly two years!

Watch out!

Family life is dangerous for the praying mantis, a type of insect. The mum is bigger than the dad – and she often eats him!

Why do baby animals play?

Lots of baby animals, such as otter pups, love to play. It helps them grow stronger and learn skills they will need as adults. Play fighting and chasing helps young animals learn how to hunt and catch prey.

Otter pups

Which bird makes the biggest nest?

The bald eagle makes the biggest nest of any bird. The largest ever seen was about 6 metres deep — big enough for a giraffe to hide in! The eagles use the same nest every year and add more sticks to it each time.

Bald eagle in its nest

Biggest egg
The ostrich lays the biggest egg of any bird. It weighs more than 1.5 kg — that's the same as 24 hen's eggs!

Are baby snakes dangerous?

Some are, yes. Not all types of snake use venom to kill their prey, but those that do, such as rattlesnakes, can give a deadly bite soon after they are born.

Ask
Find out how much you weighed at birth and measure out the same amount using weighing scales.

where do baby rabbits live?

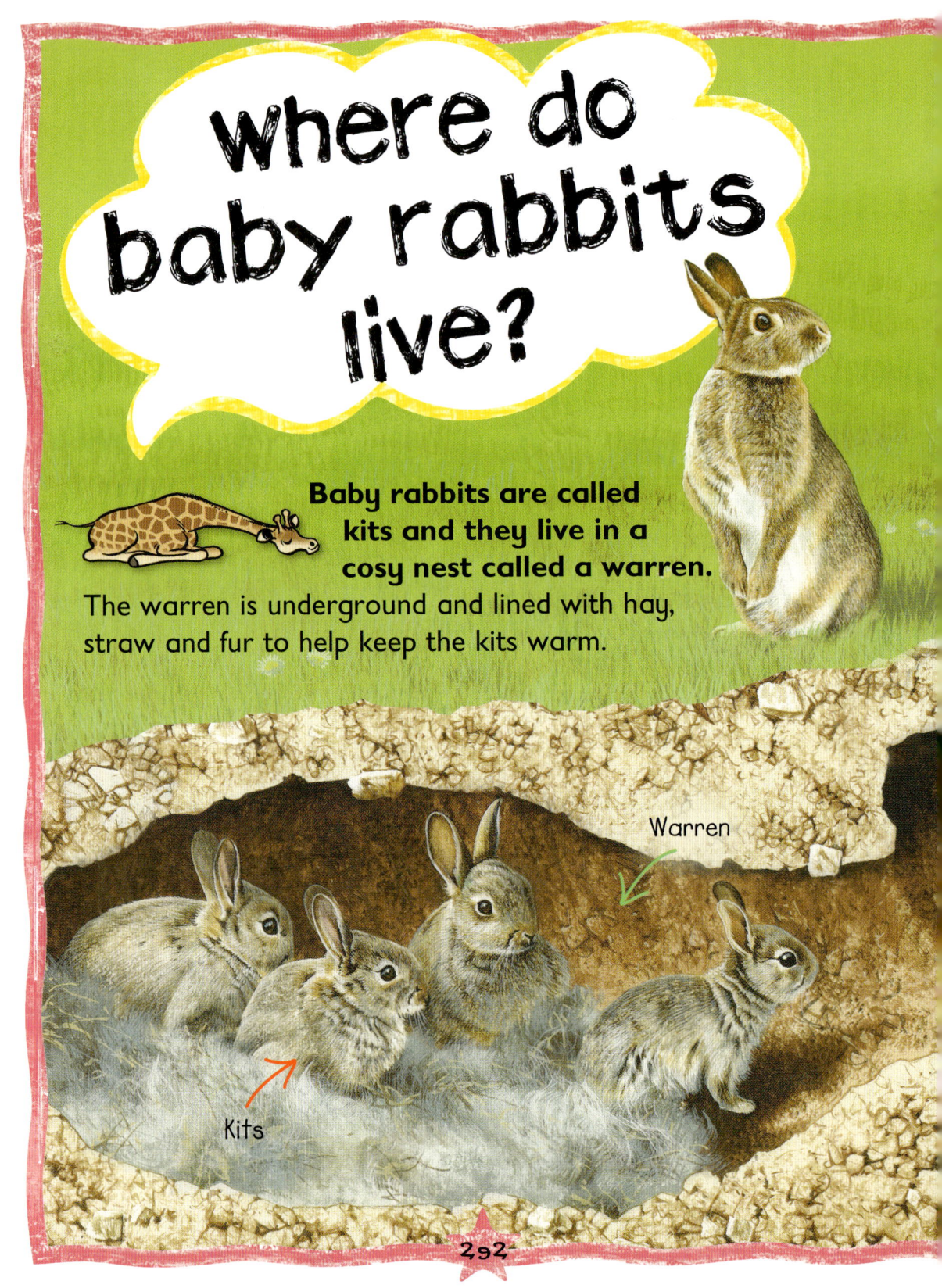

Baby rabbits are called kits and they live in a cosy nest called a warren. The warren is underground and lined with hay, straw and fur to help keep the kits warm.

Warren

Kits

When can foals walk?

Just a few hours after they are born! Foals need to be able to walk soon after birth, as in the wild they may have to escape from animals that might hunt them. Foals also stay close to their mums for safety.

Foal

Greedy!
Caterpillars spend all their time eating and can grow to more than 30,000 times the size they were when they hatched!

Draw
What does your favourite baby animal look like? Once you have decided, draw a picture.

Do baby animals laugh?

Some do! Gorillas, chimps and orang-utans laugh when they're playing or tickling each other, just like we do. Scientists think that some other animals, such as dogs, may also laugh.

How do polar bear cubs keep warm?

Polar bear cubs

Polar bears live in the Arctic, where it is always very cold. The mother bear digs a den under the snow where her cubs are born. They live there until they are three months old. It is surprisingly warm and cosy in the den!

Play
Would you be a good mum or dad? Pretend your teddy bear is a baby and look after it carefully all day.

① Caterpillar hatches from its egg

② Pupa is formed

③ Butterfly breaks out of its pupa

When do caterpillars become butterflies?

When a caterpillar has grown as big as it can, it stops eating and makes a hard case around itself called a pupa. Inside the pupa the caterpillar's body changes into a butterfly. The butterfly then breaks out of the pupa and flies away.

④ Butterfly flies away

Big baby

Blue whales have the world's biggest babies. They are about 8 metres long at birth – that's roughly as long as two cars!

Why do scorpions carry their young?

Scorpions carry their babies on their backs until they are big and strong enough to take care of themselves. They climb onto their mum's back when they hatch and are carried around for the first two weeks.

When can squirrels leave their nests?

Baby squirrels are born tiny and helpless with very little fur. They stay in their tree trunk nest for seven to ten weeks, feeding and growing. By ten weeks they are nearly fully grown and can look after themselves.

Mother and baby squirrels

Why do spiders leave home?

Baby spiders are called spiderlings, and as they grow they need to move to new areas to find food. Each spider spins silken threads from the tip of its body. These catch the air like kites and carry the spider to a new home.

Think
Try to think of different animals that make nests and draw pictures of them.

Tall tales
Giraffes are the tallest of all animals. Even a newborn giraffe is around 1.8 metres tall – that's as big as a grown-up person!

Shark egg

Do sharks lay eggs?

Some sharks do. Each egg grows in a strong case, sometimes called a mermaid's purse. The case has long threads that attach to seaweed or rocks to help keep it safe.

Shark pup

Egg case

Do sloths give birth upside down?

Yes, they do! Sloths give birth to their babies hanging upside down from trees! The baby then stays close to its mother, clinging to her fur for the first nine months of its life.

Sloth mother and baby

Make
Use some play dough to make a bird's nest and then make some little eggs to place inside.

How do penguin chicks keep warm?
Penguins usually live in cold places and keep warm by huddling together – the chicks stand on their parents feet. The penguins keep swapping places so each gets a turn at being in the middle – the warmest spot.

Queen bee
A queen honeybee lays all the eggs for her hive but she doesn't look after them. The worker bees take care of the babies for her!

Mother bird and chick

How do baby birds get food?
Most baby birds are fed by their parents. Adult birds work very hard to find tasty morsels to bring back to their chicks. The babies always seem to be hungry and wait with their beaks wide open.

Do baby elephants leave their herd?

Only male elephants ever leave their close family groups, called herds. Young elephants stay with their mums for many years. The males will eventually leave and live alone or with other males, but females stay with their herd.

Elephant mother

Calf

Make
Find lots of pictures of baby animals. Stick them on a big sheet of paper to make a poster.

How does a chick get out of its egg?

A baby bird has a tiny spike, called an egg tooth, on its beak. When it is ready to hatch, the chick makes a little hole in the shell with the egg tooth and then struggles out.

Chick breaking out

Egg

Busy mum

Virginia opossums can have up to 13 babies at a time. The babies are tiny at birth and stay with their mum for about three months.

Do badgers keep their nests clean?

Yes they do. Badgers live in underground nests called setts, and use grass, leaves and straw for bedding. The badgers bring their bedding out of the sett to air it and then throw out old, dirty bedding.

Why do lion cubs play fight?

To practise the hunting skills they have learnt from their mothers. Female lions train their cubs to hunt by bringing small animals for the cubs to catch. Then the young lions go and watch their mothers hunting from a safe distance.

Lion cubs play fighting

① Baby snake breaking eggshell

② Fully hatched

Do snakes lay eggs?

Most snakes do lay eggs, although some give birth to live babies. A snake's eggshell is tough, bendy and almost watertight, unlike a hen's egg. Female snakes usually lay about five to 20 eggs at a time.

Big mouth
The mouth brooder fish keeps its eggs safe in its mouth while they develop and grow.

Why are some eggs pear-shaped?

A guillemot is a type of sea bird that nests on cliffs. Its eggs are pear-shaped with one end more pointed than the other. This shape means that the egg rolls round in a circle if knocked, and won't roll off the cliff.

Paint
Ask an adult to hard-boil some eggs for you. Then paint pictures on the shells.

when do fox cubs leave their dens?

Fox cubs are born blind and helpless so they stay in their dens for the first few weeks. If their home is disturbed, the mother fox may move her cubs to a new den. Most cubs make their first outing when they are four weeks old.

Fox cubs

Why do cuckoos lay eggs quickly?

Because they lay their eggs in other birds' nests, instead of making their own. The other bird then looks after and feeds the cuckoo chick. A cuckoo lays an egg in just nine seconds — most birds take several minutes!

Clever baby

A gorilla baby develops more quickly than a human baby. They can crawl at about two months and walk at nine months.

Think

When human babies want their parents they cry. What noise do you think a baby bird makes to get attention?

Which bird has the safest nest?

The female hornbill makes her nest in a tree hole. The male then blocks up the hole with mud so that she and the eggs are safe from **hunters**. He leaves a hole for her beak so he can **feed her** while she's inside.

Male hornbill feeding female

When can cheetah cubs live alone?

Cheetah cubs can live alone when they are about 18 months old. Before they are ready to leave their mother they must learn to catch their own food. They learn how to hunt by watching their mother.

Cheetah cubs

Why are harp seal pups white?

Harp seals live in the snowy Arctic. The pups have white coats to keep them hidden from polar bears, which hunt them. Their fluffy coats also help to keep the seal pups warm.

Harp seal pup

What do baby pandas eat?

A baby panda drinks its mother's milk until it is about nine months old. Adult pandas feed on bamboo, and the baby starts to eat this when it is about six months old.

Discover
Some baby wasps feed on dung – animal poo! Find out what some other baby animals like to eat.

Marvellous mum
An octopus is a great mum. She guards her eggs for about a month while they grow, and she doesn't even leave them to find food.

can rhino mums be fierce?

Yes they can – a rhino mum can be fierce when she's looking after her young. If hyenas or other animals try to attack her baby, she charges towards them with her sharp horn to scare them away.

Rhino mum and calf

Are baby hedgehogs born prickly?

Luckily for hedgehog mums, their babies' have very soft spines at first. They harden as the baby grows until they are extremely sharp and strong.

Find out
Ask your parents how old you were when you could first crawl, walk and talk.

Are alligators good parents?

Alligator dads do nothing for their babies, but an alligator mum is a caring parent. She guards her eggs and helps the young to hatch. The mum may then gently lift the tiny babies in her mouth and carry them to water.

Keep warm
The Australian mallee fowl lays its eggs in a mound of earth and leaves. The bird checks the temperature with its beak to make sure its eggs stay warm.

Baby alligator

Quiz time

Do you remember what you have read about baby animals? Here are some questions to test your memory. The pictures will help you. If you get stuck, read the pages again.

3. Are baby snakes dangerous?
page 291

4. When can foals walk? 
page 293

1. Why do fawns have spots?
page 286

5. Why do scorpions carry their young?
page 295

2. Are turtles born in the sea? 
page 289

6. Do sharks lay eggs?
page 297

310

7. Do sloths give birth upside down?

page 298

11. Which bird has the safest nest?

page 305

8. How does a chick get out of its egg?

page 301

12. Why are harp seal pups white?

page 307

9. Do badgers keep their nests clean?

page 301

13. Can rhino mums be fierce?

page 308

10. Do snakes lay eggs?

page 303

Answers

1. To help them blend in with their forest homes
2. No, they are born on land
3. The types that have poison are, yes
4. A few hours after birth
5. To protect them from harm
6. Yes, some do
7. Yes
8. Using their egg tooth to make a hole in the shell, then struggle out
9. Yes
10. Most do, yes
11. The hornbill
12. To make them hard to spot in the snow
13. Yes they can – they charge at predators

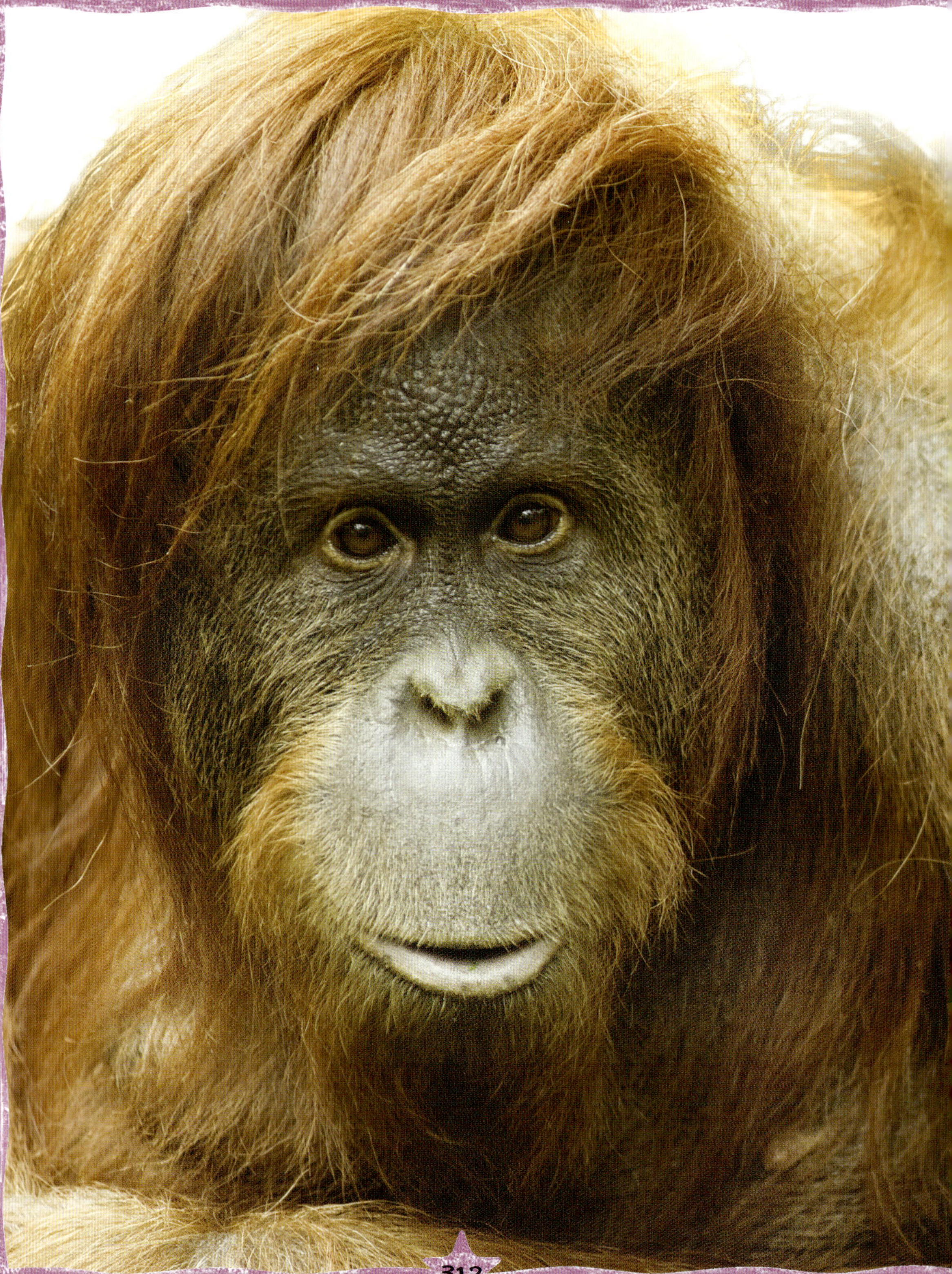

Monkeys and Apes

what is a primate?

Monkeys and apes are primates. They have big brains and are very clever. Most primates are furry. They have hands with thumbs and fingernails. Humans are primates too.

Spider monkeys

cry baby!
Bushbabies are noisy primates that live in forests. When they make loud calls to each other, they sound like crying babies.

Spell
How many words can you make using the letters in the word PRIMATE?

Are gorillas scary?
Gorillas are usually gentle animals. However they can be very fierce if they have to protect their families. Males can die fighting to save their young.

Do monkeys and apes have tails?
Monkeys have tails, but apes don't. Tails help monkeys to climb and keep their balance. Apes are usually larger than monkeys and they also have bigger brains. Gorillas, chimpanzees (chimps), bonobos, orang-utans, gibbons and humans are apes.

Orang-utan

Do primates stay awake all night?

Nocturnal primates do! Animals that are nocturnal sleep during the day and wake up at sunset. Tarsiers have big eyes to help them see in the dark. They can turn their heads right round, so they can see what's behind them.

← Tarsier

Do bonobos like to play?

Bonobos love to play! Some bonobos living in a zoo play their own game of 'blind man's bluff'! They cover their eyes and try to walk without bumping into things.

Play
Ask a grown-up to help you set up a game of 'blind man's bluff' with your friends.

Which lemur has a stripy tail?

Ring-tailed lemurs have long, bushy tails with black-and-white stripes. The males have smelly tails, and when they fight they wave them at each other.

Ring-tailed lemur

Hold tight!
Lemurs run and jump through trees. Babies have to grip tightly to their mothers' fur so they don't fall off!

317

Why do chimps lick sticks?

Because they get covered with juicy termites! Chimps poke sticks into big termite nests. The insects swarm over the sticks, which the chimps then pull out so they can lick up the tasty termites.

Chimps →

Sign
Use the Internet to discover how to sign for 'drink' and 'thank you'.

Greedy monkey!
Barbary macaques have large cheek pouches. When they find food, they stuff it into their pouches and save it for later.

Do chimps like to chatter?

Some do! A chimp called Washoe learnt how to use sign language to talk. She used her hands to make signs for lots of words, such as 'drink' and 'food'.

Squirrel monkey

Why do monkeys sleep in trees?

Monkeys can hide in a tree's branches, so they feel safer in trees than on the ground. Animals that want to eat other animals are called predators. The predators of squirrel monkeys include eagles, baboons and prickly porcupines.

Do apes love their mums?

Yes! All ape babies need their mums to look after them, but orang-utan babies need their mums the most. They are looked after by their mothers until they are about eight years old. That's longer than any other primate, apart from humans.

Orang-utan and baby

Why does an aye-aye have a long finger?

An aye-aye has a long finger to get to tasty grubs. These little primates tap trees with their fingers. If they hear a grub moving inside, they make a hole and pull it out with their extra-long middle finger.

← Aye-aye

What a racket!
Some mangabeys make a 'honk-bark' noise. Others 'whoop' to call each other and make a 'gobble' sound to say who they are.

Why do orang-utans climb trees?

Orang-utans climb trees to play amongst the branches, to find fruit to eat and to stay safe. Predators such as tigers, leopards and crocodiles hunt orang-utans.

Make
Who looks after you? Create them a beautiful card to say 'thank you'.

Why do chimps kiss?

Chimps can be very loving to members of their family. They like to sit together and kiss, stroke and groom each other. If chimps are annoyed they cough, but if they are very angry they bark, cry and scream.

Chimps

Do primates use tools?

Some primates use tools to help them get food. Capuchin monkeys use heavy rocks to crack open hard nuts. Apes can use tools too, and they even teach each other how to use rocks to open nuts.

Brown capuchin

Time for change!
People love to watch chimps. Sadly, some chimps are taken from the wild to be put in zoos or even sold as pets.

Discover
Use books and the Internet to find other animals that use tools.

When do baboons show off?

Male baboons love to show off when there are females about. They swagger around to show off their big muscles, long fangs and fine fur.

323

Do primates help forests to grow?

Yes they do! By eating plants and fruits, primates shape the trees and bushes. They also spread plant seeds in their poo. Primate poo puts goodness into the soil and helps new plants to grow.

Macaque

Why is a slow loris slow?

A slow loris likes to take life at a gentle pace. Moving slowly saves energy, so you don't need to find lots of food. It also helps an animal to stay hidden from predators.

Slow loris

Race
Have a slow race with a friend. The last person to finish is the winner!

Watch out bugs!
Slow-moving primates can creep up on their prey, such as insects, and pounce at the last second.

When do monkeys fall out of trees?

When they get too greedy! Bird eggs are a special treat for primates. Smart birds build their nests on slender branches where monkeys can't reach them.

How fast can a gibbon swing?

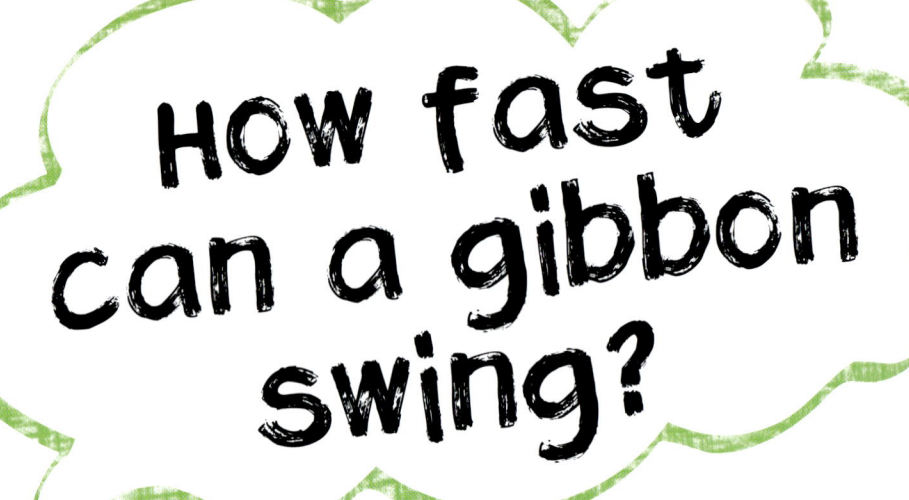

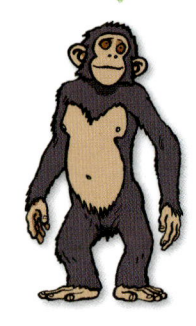

Gibbons move faster than any other primate. They can swing through trees at great speed – up to 56 kilometres an hour. Gibbons can cover up to 15 metres in just one swing.

Gibbons

Crab-eating macaque

Do monkeys eat crabs?

Some monkeys will eat almost anything they can find! Crab-eating macaques live in swamps and they will grab crabs and frogs out of shallow water. Sometimes they just drop into the cool water for a swim.

Do primates have hands and feet like us?

Instead of paws and claws, primates have fingers, toes and flat fingernails just like us. This means they can grab hold of branches and delicately pinch small things.

Count
If one macaque can catch five crabs, how many can three macaques catch?

Super movers!
Spider monkeys are some of the fastest primate climbers. They have very long arms, legs and tails.

Which monkey stays up all night?

The owl monkey, or night monkey, is nocturnal, which means it is active at night and rests during the day. Owl monkeys can see very well in the dark, thanks to their huge eyes, but they are colour-blind.

Owl monkey

Why do chimps pull faces?

Chimps pull faces to show how they are feeling. They pout when they want attention, open their lips when they are playful and bare their teeth when they are worried.

Pout
Try out some chimp faces in front of a mirror. Make an angry face too.

Pouting face

Worried face

Play face

Go wild!
Beautiful golden tamarins were once popular zoo animals, but now they are being released back into the wild so they can live free.

Which monkey has a moustache?

Emperor tamarins have big white moustaches. Other tamarins have golden fur, crowns of white hair, beards or hairy ears. Tamarins live in South America.

Do monkeys change colour?

Silvered langurs do! These monkeys have silver-grey fur, but their babies are born bright orange. After three months, grey fur begins to grow. No one knows why the babies are orange, but it may remind older monkeys to be gentle with them.

Silvered langur

Silvered langur baby

Which ape has a colourful bottom?

A healthy male mandrill baboon has a brightly coloured bottom. Their bald bottoms have blue, pink or lilac skin. Female baboons often have pink or bright red bottoms.

A handy tail!
Monkeys use their tails like an extra arm or leg. They can hang from branches using their tails.

Sifaka

Why does a sifaka skip?

Skipping is a fast way for sifakas (a type of lemur) to travel. They stand upright, with their arms stretched out, and skip sideways, scooting across the ground. Sifakas stick their tails out so they don't fall over as they hop, bound and leap.

Imagine
Pretend to be a sifaka and skip about!

How big is a gorilla?

Adult male gorillas are very big. They are called silverbacks, and they are up to 180 centimetres in height and weigh about 300 kilograms. That's the same weight as almost four people!

Silverback gorilla

Measure
Use a measuring tape to find out how tall a gorilla is.

What is the ugliest monkey?

Red uakaris (say: wak-ar-ees) are one of the ugliest monkeys. When they are born, baby uakaris have grey faces, but they turn bright red as they get older.

Bathtime fun!

Suryia the orang-utan lives in a wildlife park. He loved splashing in the bath and was taken to a pool. Suryia can now swim underwater!

Red uakari

Why do gorillas beat their chests?

When a silverback gorilla stands up and beats his chest, it is time to get away fast! This is his way of warning you that he is getting angry and might attack.

How do bonobos keep clean?

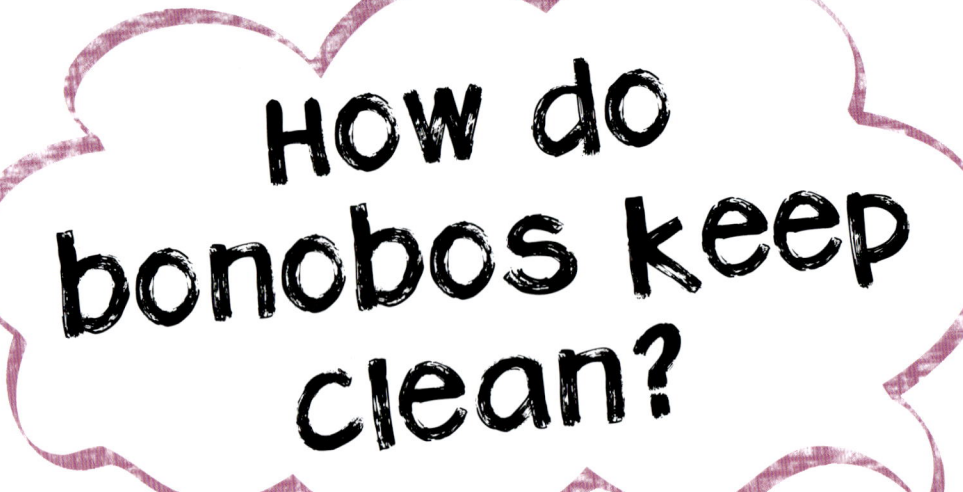

Bonobos spend lots of time cleaning each other's fur. They pick out bits of dirt, dead skin and even insects. This is called grooming and it is an important way for apes to make friends.

Bonobos

Do baboons have manes?

Male hamadryas baboons have large manes of hair that make them look big. Ancient Egyptians thought the silver-white manes made the baboons look sacred, or holy.

Scoop and sip!
Some baboons dig holes by ponds and let water flow into them. The water is clean enough to drink, with no nasty bugs in it.

Think
Can you think of any other animals that have manes of hair or fur?

Which orang-utan is in a film?

King Louie is one of the cartoon stars of a Disney film called *The Jungle Book*. He loves to sing, dance and play practical jokes. The story is based in an Indian jungle, but orang-utans don't really live in India.

King Louie

Baloo

Which monkey has a big nose?

In Southeast Asia there are small monkeys with big noses. They are called proboscis monkeys (say: prob-os-kis), because proboscis is another word for 'nose'. The males have the biggest noses of all. When they run, their noses flop up and down!

Proboscis monkeys

Make
Use card and coloured pens to create a monkey mask.

Why do De Brazza's monkeys have white beards?

To scare other monkeys! De Brazza's monkeys also have long fangs. When they open their mouths wide, the white beards and long teeth make them look scary.

De Brazza's monkey

Go ape!
Every year, people all over the world dress up as gorillas and run 7 kilometres. They raise money to save the few gorillas that still live in the wild.

How do orang-utans stay dry?

Orang-utans live in tropical forests where it rains a lot every day. These clever apes use big leaves like umbrellas, and hold them over their heads to keep dry!

How do monkeys keep warm?

Most monkeys live in warm places. Japanese macaques live in mountainous areas where the weather can turn very cold. They keep warm by soaking in pools of hot water that bubble up from the ground.

Japanese macaques

Why do bushbabies leap?

Bushbabies leap to catch their prey. They are fast movers, and can even take scorpions and spiders by surprise. In just one leap, a bushbaby can cover 10 metres!

Bushbaby

Lucky for some!
Only some lucky Japanese macaques have hot springs to soak in. Others have to huddle together to keep warm when cold winds bring snow.

Think
Can you work out how many metres a bushbaby would cover in three leaps?

Which primate has two tongues?

Bushbabies use two tongues to eat gum, which comes from trees. They use their teeth to scrape the gum from the bark, then wipe it off their teeth with the special second tongue.

Quiz time

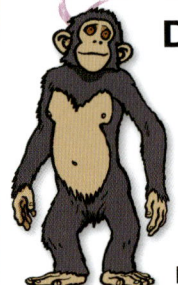

Do you remember what you have read about monkeys and apes? Here are some questions to test your memory. The pictures will help you. If you get stuck, read the pages again.

3. Why do chimps lick sticks?

page 318

4. Why does an aye-aye have a long finger?

page 321

1. Are gorillas scary?

page 315

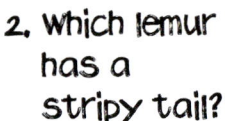

page 323

5. When do baboons show off?

2. Which lemur has a stripy tail?

page 317

6. Why is a slow loris slow?

page 325

340

7. Do monkeys eat crabs?
page 327

8. Which monkey has a moustache?
page 329

9. Why does a sifaka skip?
page 331

10. What is the ugliest monkey?
page 333

11. Do baboons have manes?
page 335

12. Which monkey has a big nose?
page 336

13. How do monkeys keep warm?
page 338

Answers

1. Gorillas are usually gentle, but they can be fierce when they protect their families
2. The ring-tailed lemur
3. Because they get covered with termites when chimps poke them into big termite nests
4. To get to tasty grubs in trees
5. When there are females about
6. To save energy and stay hidden from predators
7. Crab-eating macaques do
8. An emperor tamarin
9. Skipping is a fast way for them to travel
10. The red uakari
11. Male hamadryas baboons do
12. The proboscis monkey
13. Japanese macaques keep warm by soaking in pools of hot water that bubble up from the ground

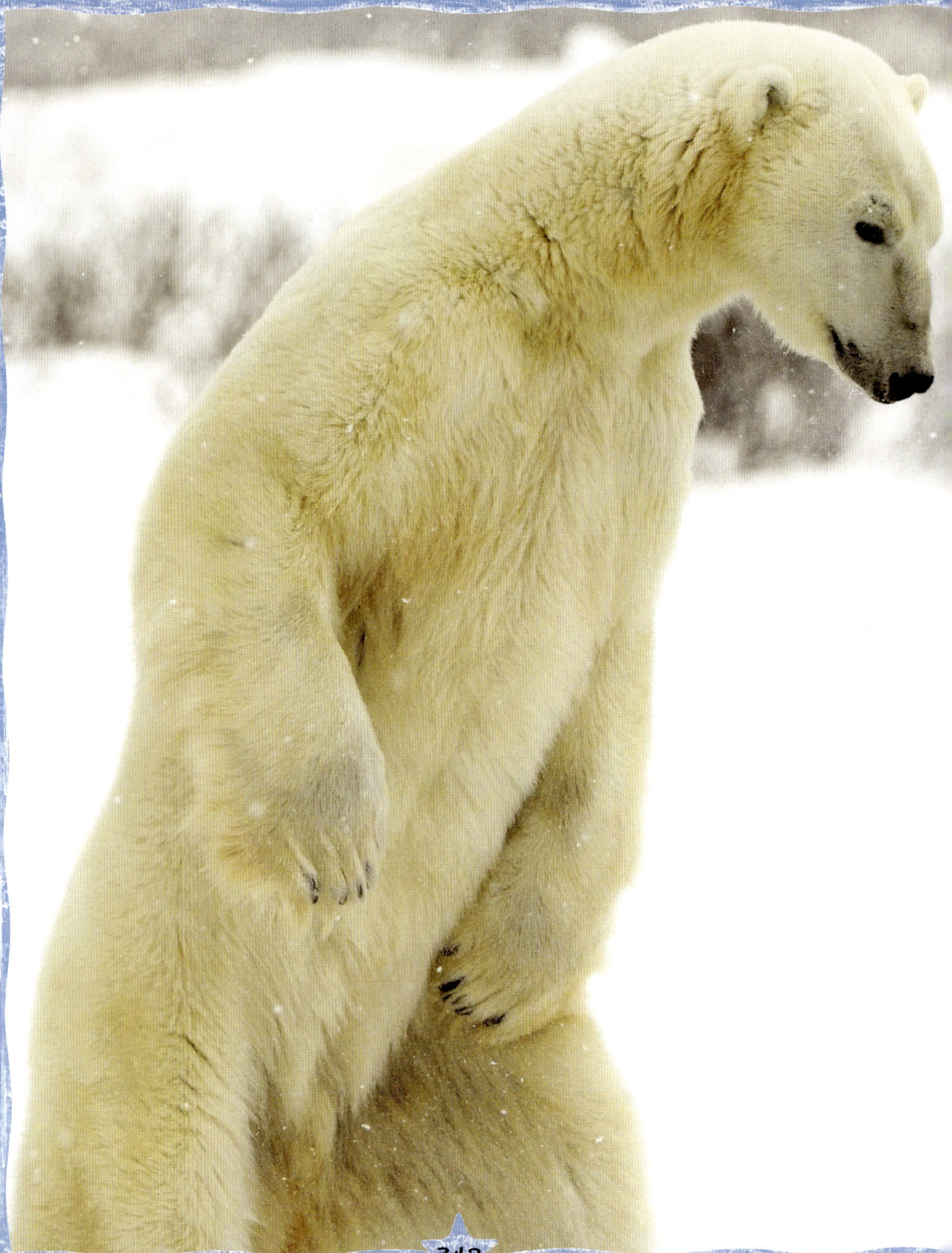

Deadly Creatures

Why do hippos attack each other?

Male hippos attack each other to defend the patch of land where they live. When they fight, hippos stand face-to-face with their mouths wide-open, and slash and swipe at each other with their tusk-like teeth. Sometimes these fights end in the death of one, or both of the hippos.

Hippos

344

Which bird can kill while it flies?

Lots of birds hunt 'on the wing'. The peregrine falcon is the fastest hunting animal in the world and dives at 230 kilometres an hour. It chases its prey before attacking it to tire it out.

Peregrine falcon

Hold it, hippopotamus!

Hippos and whales are closely related – maybe this is why hippos can hold their breath under water for 12 minutes!

Do army ants go hunting?

Army ants hunt in groups, sometimes of more than one million ants. They move forward in a wave across the ground. Ants at the front of the group kill insects and small lizards in their path, while ants further back carry food to the nest.

Army ants

Explore
Ants live in most places, even in your garden. Take a look outside and see if you can spot any.

Why do snakes have fangs?

Poisonous snakes such as rattlesnakes have an extra-long pair of teeth called fangs. A deadly poison called venom runs along a groove in each fang. When the snake bites an animal, its fangs sink into the animal's skin and venom is injected.

Rattlesnake

Which creature kills with its tail?

All scorpions have a poisonous sting in their tail. They use their front claw-like arms to hold their prey, while their tail-sting injects a harmful venom. Few scorpions can badly injure a human, but a sting from the death stalker scorpion can kill.

Common yellow scorpion

Death match!
Scorpions normally live alone because most of them eat other scorpions. If two scorpions meet, they will fight to the death and the loser is eaten by the winner.

Why are eels shocking?

Electric eels use electricity to zap their prey and to attack other animals that threaten them. The electric eel, which is actually a type of fish, can produce up to 600 volts of electricity — enough to kill a human!

Discover
Some eels use electricity to hunt. What things in your home use electricity?

When can stones be deadly?

When they are fish. The stonefish looks just like a piece of coral-covered rock or stone on the seabed. It sits and waits for its prey to come close. Then the stonefish strikes out at lightning speed and gobbles up its victim. For defence, the stonefish is covered in poisonous spikes.

Stonefish

Hornet

Can insects be deadly?

Many insects can harm other animals. Bees, wasps and hornets have stings in their tails that can inject venom. A sting from one of these insects can cause swelling and pain, and, rarely, even death.

King sting!
The world's largest hornet is the Asian giant hornet. Its body is up to 4.5 centimetres long and its stinger is 6 millimetres long.

Remember
If you are stung by an insect tell an adult straight away because some stings can make you feel unwell.

What do animals use their tusks for?

Tusks are overgrown teeth, and animals such as walruses and elephants use their tusks as weapons to stab and swipe at attackers. Males use them to fight one another during the mating season.

Why do crocodiles have big teeth?

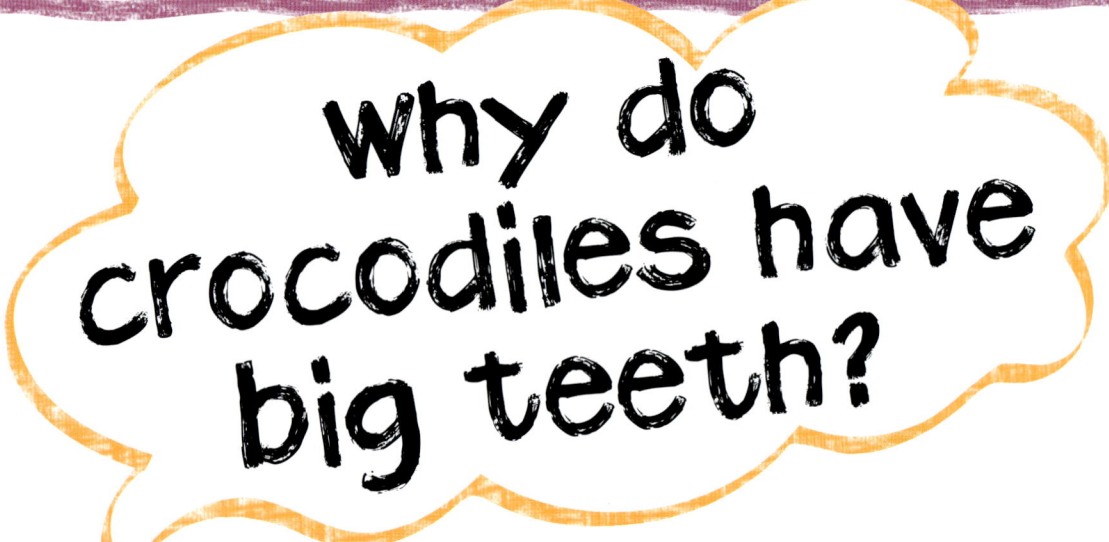

Crocodiles have lots of big teeth for catching their prey. A crocodile's diet includes fish, birds and mammals, such as gazelle and wildebeest. The crocodile's sharp teeth and powerful jaws help it to keep hold of its prey and to bite chunks off to swallow.

Nile crocodile

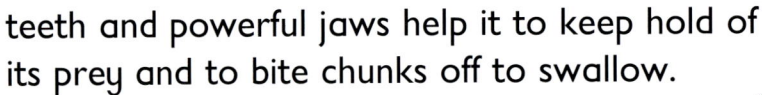

Do snakes eat people?

Pythons, such as Burmese pythons, have been known to attack and kill humans – but rarely. These snakes usually eat small mammals and birds, but can open their mouths wide enough to swallow animals such as pigs and deer whole!

Burmese python

Boiled eggs!
Whether a baby crocodile is a female or a male depends on temperature. A female will develop in a warm egg and a male will develop in a cool egg.

Make
Using an old sock for the body, buttons for eyes and wooden pegs for teeth, make a crocodile glove puppet.

Gazelle

What is a deathspin?

A deathspin is what crocodiles and alligators do to drown their prey. A crocodile pulls its victim underwater and twists and turns until the animal is dead. The crocodiles' strong jaws keep a grip on the animal as it rolls and turns in the water.

what is a black widow?

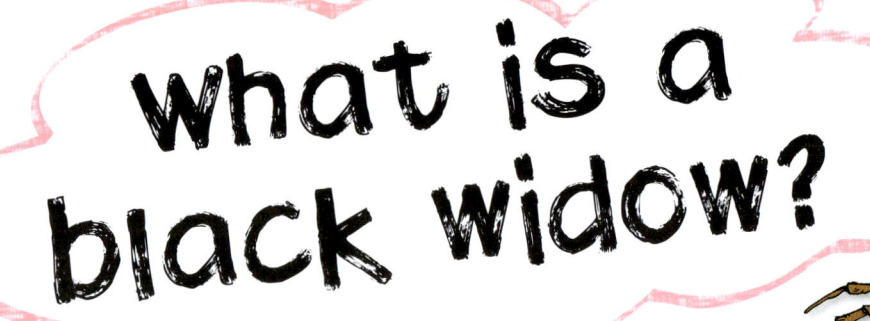

The black widow is one of the world's most deadly spiders. Black widows only bite if they are disturbed. Male black widows are harmless, but a bite from a female can kill a human. Sometimes, the female black widow eats the male after mating.

Black widow

Think
Lots of people are scared of spiders. Are there any creepy-crawlies that you are afraid of?

Why do fish bite?

Piranhas are small fish with razor-sharp teeth. They can be very fierce and will bite anything that they think they can eat. Piranhas usually hunt alone but may gather in groups to attack larger animals, which they strip to the bone in minutes.

Piranhas feeding

A bite to eat!

Piranhas are found in rivers in South America and are often caught for food by the local people. Their teeth are used in weapons and tools.

Why do crocodiles eat rotting meat?

Crocodiles eat rotting meat because it is easier to swallow. Crocodiles and alligators store their food by wedging the dead animal under an underwater branch or log, so that it rots down. Sometimes, they store their food for several weeks.

Which bat eats bones?

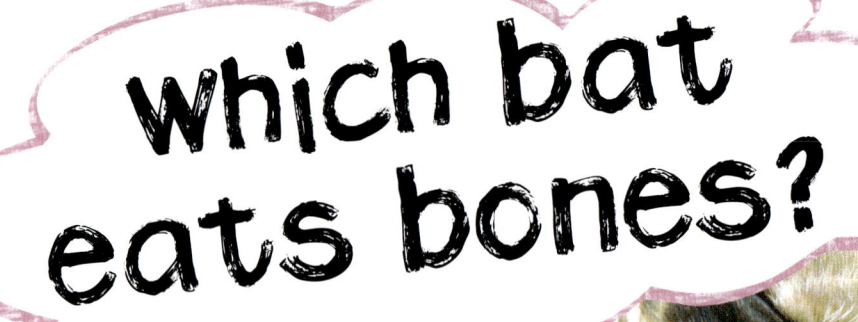

False vampire bats kill their prey by biting its head or neck and crushing its skull. Then it swallows the flesh, bones, teeth, fur and even feathers of its prey. Its favourite foods are birds, as well as lizards, frogs and mice.

False vampire bat

Flies for tea!
Most bats eat insects. They catch their prey by snatching it out of the air while flying. Some bats will catch around 2000 insects in one night!

Which tiny jellyfish is deadly?

The Irukandji jellyfish can be found in the waters around Australia. It is very dangerous despite its small size – its body is the size of a small grape and its tentacles can give a deadly sting.

Irukandji jellyfish

Poison-dart frog

Why are some frogs brightly coloured?

Poison-dart frogs are brightly coloured to tell attackers to stay away. Some kinds of these frogs also make a poisonous slime on their skin. Local people of South America wipe the poison onto the ends of their hunting darts because it's strong enough to kill animals such as monkeys.

Wear
Try on some colourful, bright clothes, like the poison-dart frog. How many colours are in your outfit?

What is the deadliest lizard?

The Komodo dragon is the deadliest, and biggest, meat-eating lizard. It eats every part of an animal, including its bones. This lizard has a poisonous bite, so even if prey escapes, the Komodo dragon just follows it until it weakens and dies.

Komodo dragon

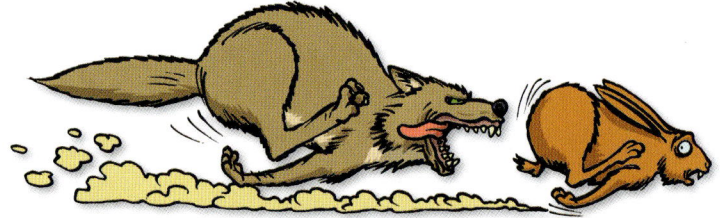

How do coyotes catch their prey?

Coyotes are fast runners and often chase speedy jackrabbits across rocks and up hills. When hunting larger animals such as deer, a group of coyotes chase the animal to tire it out and bite its neck to stop it breathing.

Anaconda

LOOK
Snakes open their mouths very wide to eat big animals. Look in a mirror and see how wide you can open yours.

Why do snakes squeeze their prey?

Some snakes, such as anacondas, squeeze their prey to death instead of using poison. These snakes are called constrictors. The captured animal is squeezed tighter and tighter until it can't breathe. Then the snake swallows it whole!

Deadly down under!

Australia has more poisonous snakes for its size than any other country – including eight of the world's ten deadliest snakes.

Can monkeys be dangerous?

Mandrills are the biggest type of monkey, and they can be dangerous. Their fangs grow up to 7 centimetres long and are used as deadly weapons to attack weaker members of their group. Males also show their teeth to impress females during the mating season.

Draw
Using colouring pencils, draw a picture of a monkey. See if you can make it as colourful as this mandrill.

Mandrill

Why do wolves snarl?

Wolves snarl when they are angry or threatened by another animal. When a wolf snarls, its lips curl back to show its long, sharp teeth and its nostrils widen. The fur on the wolf's back also stands on end to make it look bigger to an attacker.

Wolf

Scary sound!

A wolf's growl is a very low, deep sound. They growl to threaten other wolves and to show they have power over a group of wolves, which is called a pack.

Which shark gives a warning before it bites?

The grey reef shark does. If it feels threatened it drops its fins down and raises its snout so that its body is in an 'S' shape. Then it weaves and rolls through the water. If its warning is not taken, the shark will bite before swimming away.

Which big cats hunt in teams?

Unlike most big cats, lions hunt as a team. Female lions, called lionesses, hunt for food while the males and cubs wait for their meal. A group of lionesses can catch large animals, including zebra, gazelle and wildebeest.

Lionesses hunting

Which turtle has a deadly bite?

The alligator snapping turtle does. It has a 'beak' made of a tough material. It eats fish, which it lures in with its worm-like tongue, as well as crabs, clams and even other turtles!

Alligator snapping turtle

When are brown bears deadly?

Brown bears can be deadly if they are injured or weak, or if they are surprised by a human. A mother bear will also defend her cubs by attacking. In North America, a number of people have been killed by brown bears.

Think
Bears can be scary! Try to think of any friendly bears that appear in films and cartoons.

Deadly lure!
The alligator snapping turtle lures its prey into its mouth by wiggling its pink tongue!

361

Which owl hunts other owls?

Eagle owl

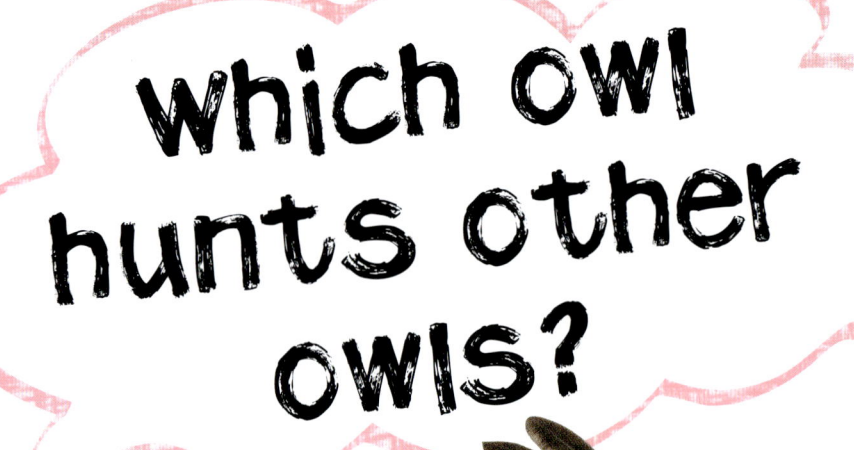

The eagle owl does. Eagle owls hunt 'on the wing' (while flying) for any kind of bird, including other owls. As well as hunting in the air, these owls hunt on the ground for insects, reptiles and mammals. The eagle owl is the biggest owl.

What do fleas eat?

Fleas live on most furry animals, and sometimes humans. They jump from animal to animal feeding on blood and can spread disease. Fleas were responsible for spreading the 'black death', a disease that killed millions of people in the 14th century.

Flea

What is the deadliest octopus?

The blue-ringed octopus is the world's most dangerous octopus – and it's only 10 to 20 centimetres long. It grabs prey with its sticky tentacles and then gives a bite that injects venom. Its venom is strong enough to kill a human in four minutes!

Blue-ringed octopus

Silent hunter!

An owl's feathers have fluffy edges. This softens the sound of their wings flapping so they can swoop down on their prey in silence.

Count

An octopus has eight tentacles. How many tentacles would three octopuses have?

How do funnel web spiders kill?

Funnel web spiders are poisonous and have large fangs that are strong enough to bite through your fingernail. They bite their prey many times, injecting a strong poison until their victim is dead. Funnel web spiders normally eat insects and small lizards.

Funnel web spider

Fighting elephants

When are elephants deadly?

During the breeding season, male elephants, called bulls, become aggressive and fight each other to win a female. One elephant is strong enough to flip over a car.

web-tastic!

There are about 20,000 types of spider that spin webs to catch their prey. Most of these make a new web every night, after they've eaten the old one!

Which poisonous fish is spiky?

The pufferfish puffs itself up into a spiky ball when attacked. It gulps in water to make its body swell and its spikes stand on end. It contains deadly poison but some chefs are trained to cook it. They know which parts to take out so that it's safe to eat.

Think

Can you puff like a pufferfish? Take a deep breath in. What happens to your body?

Are polar bears friendly?

Big, fluffy polar bears look friendly, but they are deadly killers. Young polar bears practise fighting skills to get ready for battles as adults over females. The bear's powerful bite and huge paws means it can kill its prey quickly.

Polar bears fighting

Which reptile squirts poison?

If attacked, the fire salamander squirts out a poison that is harmful to other animals. Fire salamanders look like a cross between a lizard and a frog, and they have colourful patterns on their skin to warn predators that they are poisonous.

Fire salamander

Burning hot!
The word 'salamander' means 'within fire' in Persian because a long time ago people thought that salamanders could walk through fire. However, this isn't true.

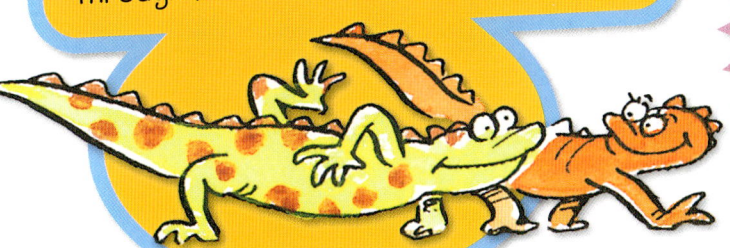

Colour
Draw an outline of a fire salamander and colour it in using five colours.

Why do rhinos charge?

Female rhinos protect their calves by charging at enemies. Rhinos have bad eyesight, but excellent senses of smell and hearing. They can quickly sense if there is a threat nearby. A charging rhino can reach a speed of 50 kilometres an hour!

Which deadly creature lives in a shell?

The cone shell is a type of snail that lives in the sea. Instead of chasing its prey, it sits and waits for creatures to come close. It has a long, tongue-like arm that it uses to shoot a poisonous dart into its victim.

Make
Using a cardboard box, make your own shell. Paint a pattern on it like the cone shell's.

Cone shell

Do killer bees really exist?

Yes, they do! A scientist tried to create bees that made more honey than normal, but instead he created 'killer bees'. They attack in large groups and around 1000 people have been killed by these minibeasts.

Delightful droppings!

Lots of insects find animal droppings delicious. Some beetles lay their eggs in steaming piles of droppings, so that when the eggs hatch, the young insects can eat the dung!

How do flies spread diseases?

Tsetse flies spread disease when they feed. They bite and suck blood from one animal and then another, leaving germs behind. These germs can cause 'sleeping sickness' in humans, which makes you want to sleep all the time.

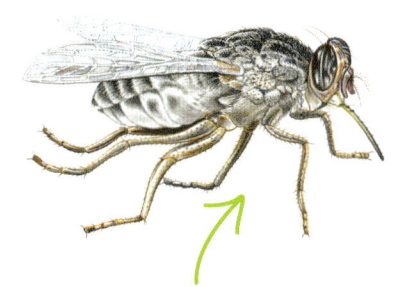

Tsetse fly before feeding

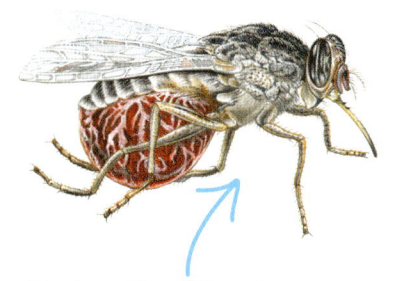

Tsetse fly after feeding

Quiz time

Do you remember what you have read about deadly creatures? These questions will test your memory. The pictures will help you. If you get stuck, read the pages again.

1. Which bird can kill while it flies?

   page 345

2. Which creature kills with its tail?

   page 347

3. When can stones be deadly?

   page 348

4. Do snakes eat people?

   page 351

5. What is a black widow?

   page 352

6. Why do crocodiles eat rotting meat?

   page 353

7. What is the deadliest lizard?

page 356

8. Which shark gives a warning before it bites?

page 359

9. Which big cats hunt in teams?

page 360

10. Which turtle has a deadly bite?

page 361

11. What is the deadliest octopus?

page 363

12. Which poisonous fish is spiky?

page 365

13. Do killer bees really exist?

page 369

Answers

1. The peregrine falcon
2. The scorpion
3. When they are a stonefish
4. Some types of python have but this is very rare
5. One of the world's deadliest spiders
6. Because it is easier to swallow
7. The Komodo dragon
8. The grey reef shark
9. Lions do
10. The alligator snapping turtle
11. The blue-ringed octopus
12. The pufferfish
13. Yes, they do

371

Index

A
acacia trees 150
acids 84
aerials 18, 19, 29
agoutis 203
aircraft 11, 13, 93
albatrosses 121, 229
algae 106, 144, 230
alligator snapping turtles 361
alligators 309, 351, 353
anacondas 357
Antarctica 90, 117
ants 150, 207, 345
apes 215, 314, 315, 320–321, 323
aqua lungs 128
Arctic 69, 122, 294, 307
army ants 345

arteries 53
Asian giant hornets 349
astronauts 69
atoms 27
auroras 95
autumn 97, 154
avalanches 91
aye-ayes 321

B
babies
 animal 189, 215, 270, 273, 277, 284–309, 320, 330, 351
 human 36–37, 50
baboons 319, 323, 331, 335
badgers 301
bald eagles 291
bamboo 159, 307
bananas 135
baobab trees 142
Barbary macaques 319
barnacles 115, 166
barracudas 231
bats 137, 209, 354
batteries 11, 17
Bay of Fundy 181

bays 174
beachcombing 181
beaches, sandy 167, 175
bears
 brown bears 361
 grizzly bears 178
 polar bears 122, 165, 294, 307, 366
 sun bears 211
Beaufort Scale 93
bees 136, 211, 299, 349, 369
beetles 171, 202, 369
Bengal tigers 275
bicycles 7, 60
big cats 200, 214, 254–279, 360
birds 87, 137, 139, 143, 157, 183, 195, 196, 205, 207, 215, 216, 273, 291, 299, 301, 345, 362
 eggs 305, 309
 flightless 203
 seabirds 120–121, 123, 170, 171, 172–173, 176, 181, 189, 229, 303
birds of paradise 205
'black death' 363

black widows 352
black-footed cats 257
black-tip reef sharks 169
blood 52, 53
blood cells 43, 53
blood-suckers 197, 363, 369
blue whales 114–115, 284, 295
blue-footed boobies 121
blue-ringed octopuses 234–235, 363
blue-spotted rays 231
blue-tailed day lizards 152
bluebells 149
bluestreak cleaner wrasses 244
bones 42–43
bonobos 315, 317, 334
boobies 121
bottlenose dolphins 231
box jellyfish 233, 239
boxer crabs 245
Boyd's dragons 210
brain coral 240
brain waves 59
brains 45, 54, 56, 58–59, 314, 315
bread 48, 149
breathing 46–47, 108, 128, 228, 285
breezes 93
brown bears 361

buds 134
bull sharks 237
Burmese pythons 351
burning 8–9, 149
bushbabies 314, 339
butterflies 140, 146, 206, 295
butterfly fish 231, 241

C

cables 16
cacao beans 199
cacti 139, 147
camels 87
camouflage 200, 211, 217, 227, 241, 260, 263, 278, 286, 307, 348
candles 9
canines 50
capuchin monkeys 323
caracals 256, 277
carbon dioxide 84
carrots 143
cars 7, 12, 24, 30, 98
Caspian Sea 81
cassowaries 203
caterpillars 141, 207, 293, 295
caves 73, 84–85
cells 39, 43, 53, 59
central processing units 21
cerebellum 58, 59
cerebrum 58

chameleons 201
cheetahs 266–267, 268, 269, 271, 306
chemicals 8, 98
chicks 120, 123, 171, 299, 301
chimneys, underwater 126
chimpanzees (chimps) 213, 293, 315, 318–319, 322, 323, 329
chocolate 199
Christmas Island red crabs 169, 187
Christmas tree worms 235
circuits 17
cirrus clouds 89
cities 12
clams 177, 243
cleaner wrasses 113, 244, 249
cliffs 175
cloud forests 212
clouded leopards 261, 271, 276
clouds 88, 89, 95
clownfish 112, 113, 236
coal 31, 99
coasts 83

cochlea 55
cockles 177
colds 56
collarbone 42
colour blindness 328
compasses 70
computers 13, 20–21, 22
concrete 13
cone shells 368
constrictors (snakes) 218, 357
Cook, James 247
coral 225, 240, 243
coral reefs 83, 112–113, 168, 182, 224–225, 229–249
core, Earth's 70, 71
cormorants 173
cotton 25
Cousteau, Jacques 126
cows 150
coyotes 356
crab-eating macaques 327
crabeater seals 165
crabs 107, 119, 168, 169, 180, 185, 187, 242, 245
craters 66
crocodiles 118, 273, 321, 350, 351, 353

crown-of-thorns starfish 249
crust, Earth's 70, 76
cubs and kittens
  cheetahs 306
  foxes 304
  lions 255, 273, 302
  pumas 270
  tigers 257, 260, 277
cuckoos 305
cucumbers 141
cumulus clouds 89
curlews 176
cuttlefish 227
cyclones 93

D

daffodils 149
day and night 68, 69, 96
De Brazza's monkeys 337
deathspin 351
deer 286
deforestation 98, 213
deltas 175
dens 294, 304
dermis 39
deserts 86, 139
dinosaurs 73, 135
diseases 363, 369

divers 128, 228, 237
dizziness 55
doctors 27, 59, 61
dogs 293
dolphins 111, 231, 241
dugongs 187
dung (poo) 307, 324, 369

E

eagle owls 362
eagles 216, 291, 319
eardrum 55
ears 11, 43, 55
Earth
  day and night 68, 69, 96
  formation 66
  layers 70–71
  magnetic field 15, 29
  protecting 98–99
  seasons 96–97
  spinning 68–69, 165
earthquakes 71, 76–77, 167
  epicentre 76
echolocation 209
ecologists 28, 29
EEG machines 59

eels 113, 244, 347
egg tooth 301
eggs
  alligators 309
  birds 120, 123, 172, 229, 291, 301, 303, 305, 309, 325
  crabs 187
  crocodiles 351
  fish 235, 287, 297, 303
  frogs 285
  insects 171, 299, 369
  lobsters 249
  octopuses 307
  snakes 303
  turtles 188, 226, 289
Egyptians, ancient 273, 335
Einstein, Albert 27
electric eels 347
electric motors 11
electric rays 247
electricity 11, 14, 16–17, 31, 59, 247
electromagnets 14
elephant seals 173
elephants 219, 287, 289, 300, 349, 365
email 22
emerald tree boas 218
emperor penguins 123
emperor tamarins 329
enamel 50
endangered animals 261
energy 8, 19, 27, 99
epicentre 76
epidermis 39
estuaries 178
exercise 60
experiments 26
extinction 261
eye of a hurricane 93
eyes 54, 127, 279, 316, 328

F

fairy penguins 123
false vampire bats 354
fangs 337, 346, 358, 364
fats 48
fawns 286
fighting 271, 315, 344, 347, 349, 358, 365, 366
fingernails 41, 314, 327
fire salamanders 367
fireflies 211
fireworks 8
fish 108–111, 113, 168, 183, 203, 232, 236, 239, 244, 245, 249, 303, 348, 353
  camouflage 227, 241, 348
  freshwater 81, 178
  poisonous 228, 248, 348, 365
  schools 108
flamingos 183
fleas 363
flies 148, 156, 201, 369
flowers 134, 136, 140, 146, 147, 149, 152, 179, 201
flying fish 109
foals 293
fogbows 95
follicles 40
food 48–49, 50, 51, 60, 124, 159
forces 6, 7
forest fires 149
fossils 72–73
foxes 181, 304
freshwater 81, 105
friction 6
frogs 207, 213, 215, 217, 285, 355
frost 155
frowning 45
fruit and vegetables 48, 159
fulmars 171
fungi 141
funnel web spiders 364
fur 255, 263, 266, 274, 323, 330, 359

G

gannets 173
gazelles 268, 350, 360
geckos 195, 219
gentoo penguins 123
germs 38, 53, 61, 369
gibbons 315, 326
gills 108, 285
giraffes 297
glaciers 78, 79
glands 269
glass 25, 31, 179
glasswort 179
gloves 38
glow-worms 211
golden poison-arrow frogs 207
golden tamarins 329
Goliath frogs 215
Goliath spiders 197
gorillas 212, 217, 293, 305, 315, 332, 333, 337
grass 153, 159, 230
grasslands 86, 265, 268, 279
gravity 7, 27
grazing animals 153, 158
Great Barrier Reef 113, 224, 247
great white sharks 110
green poison-dart frogs 285
grey reef sharks 359
grizzly bears 178
grooming 287, 322, 334
groupers 113
guillemots 170, 303
gulls 170
gum trees 157, 339

H

habitats 194
hair 40, 41, 60
hamadryas baboons 335
hammerhead sharks 246
harp seals 307
headlands 174
hearing 55
heart 45, 52–53
heartbeats 52
hedgehogs 309
Hercules beetles 202
herds 300
hermit crabs 169, 242
herring 111
hippos 344, 345
honeybees 299
hornbills 305
hornets 349
horses 293
howler monkeys 199
human body 36–61
 babies 36–37, 50
humans 314, 315
hummingbirds 87, 139, 207
humpback whales 115
hunting 259, 267, 273, 278, 290, 302, 306, 345, 360, 362
hurricane hunters 93
hurricanes 93
hyenas 279

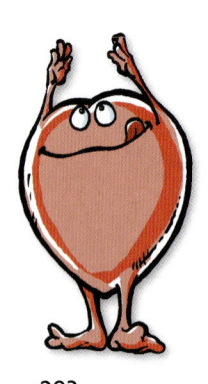

I

Iberian lynx 261
ice 78–79, 90
icebergs 79
iguanas 119, 189
illnesses 60, 61
incisors 50
insect stings 349
Internet 22–23
intertidal zone 167, 183
intestines 51

376

iron 14, 70
Irukandji jellyfish 355
islands 82, 105

J

jaguars 200, 257, 272, 273, 275
Japanese macaques 338, 339
jellyfish 119, 225, 233, 239, 355
jet engines 11
jetskis 129
joeys 288
joints 43, 44
Jungle Book, The (film) 335
junglefowl 215

K

kangaroos 204, 288
keratin 41
kidneys 53
killer bees 369
killer whales 111
kits 292
kittens 270
knee pads 38
koalas 157
Komodo dragons 356–357
krill 114

L

laboratories 26
lagoons 182, 183
lakes 81, 84
larynx 47
laughing 293
lava 75, 85, 105
leaf bugs 143
leaf insects 211
leaflitter toads 217
leafy seadragons 233
learning 37
leatherback turtles 119
leaves 134, 145, 151, 154, 207
leeches 197
lemurs 208, 209, 216, 317, 331
leopard seals 117
leopards 261, 264, 271, 272, 274, 276, 321
levers 6
light 10, 54
light bulbs 17
light rays 10
lightning 17
limestone 25
limpets 106, 166
lionfish 113, 228
lions 86, 255, 258–259, 263, 269, 273, 278, 302, 360
litters 270
lizards 119, 152, 189, 195, 201, 205, 210, 219, 356
lobsters 119, 125, 249
lungs 46, 47, 52
lynx 261, 263

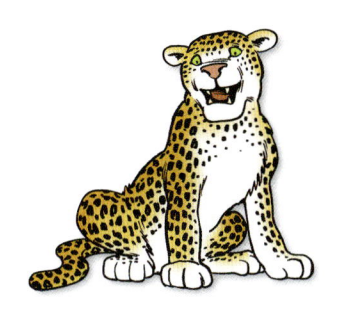

M

macaques 319, 324, 327, 338, 339
macaws 195
machines 6–7, 16, 27, 30
magma 74
magnetic fields 15, 29
magnetic poles 15
magnets 11, 14–15, 70
mallee fowl 309
manatees 187
mandrills 331, 358
mangabeys 219, 321
mangroves 171, 186
mantis shrimps 237
mantle, Earth's 70
marrow 43
materials 24–25, 26
mating 121, 205, 349, 352, 358
medicines 27, 266
mermaids 127
mermaid's purses 297

meteorites 66
microchips 21
microwaves 19
millipedes 209
mobile phones 23
modems 22
molars 50
monkeys 199, 219, 287, 314, 315, 319, 323, 324, 325, 327, 328, 329, 330, 331, 333, 336–337, 338, 355, 358
Moon 66, 67, 69, 165
moray eels 113, 244
moths 146
mountains 71, 75, 78, 82, 85, 89, 91, 105
mouth brooder fish 303
mudskippers 183
mummies 273
muscle fibres 44
muscles 44–45, 47, 48, 49, 51, 52, 54, 59
mushrooms 141
mussels 166

N

nails 41, 314, 327
narwhals 115
national parks 99
nectar 139, 140, 146
nerves 39, 44, 45, 48, 54, 59
nests 291, 305
night see day and night
Nile crocodiles 350
nocturnal animals 316, 328
North and South Poles 97, 165
Northern lights 95
noses 56, 57, 336
nuclear energy 27
nutcrackers 137
nuts 137, 203, 323

O

oarfish 109
oases 86
ocean floor 82–83
ocean parks 243
oceans and seas 67, 69, 88, 104–105
ocelots 261
octopuses 168, 185, 225, 234–235, 247, 307, 363
oesophagus 49
oil 31, 99
okapis 217
opossums 301

orang-utans 215, 217, 284, 293, 315, 320, 321, 333, 335, 337
orcas 111
ostriches 291
otters 117, 145, 181, 290
owl monkeys 328
owls 362, 363
oxygen 46, 52, 53, 108, 128
oysters 125

P

packs (animals) 359
pandas 307
paper 31, 151
paperbark trees 155
parrotfish 112, 232
parrots 195
pasta 48
pearls 125
pebbles 175
penguins 123, 165, 177, 179, 299
peregrine falcons 345
petrels 121
Philippine eagles 216

378

pine trees 153
piranhas 203, 353
pirates 239
pitcher plants 201
pivots 6
planets 66
plants 134–159
  desert plants 139
  flowers 134, 136, 140, 146, 147, 149, 152, 179, 201
  plant parts 134
  seeds 140, 141, 149, 153, 155, 157, 158, 324
plates, Earth's 71, 75
playground rides 6
playing 37, 59, 273, 290
plovers 172
plunge pools 80
poison-arrow frogs 207, 355
poisonous animals
  cone shells 368
  fire salamanders 367
  fish 228, 248, 348, 365
  frogs 207, 355
  jellyfish 233, 355
  lizards 356
  octopuses 363
  scorpions 347
  snakes 291, 346, 357
  spiders 352, 364
polar bears 122, 165, 294, 307, 366

poles, magnetic 15
pollen 136, 137, 140, 152
pollution 30, 98, 99
polyps (coral) 83, 112, 168, 224, 225, 230, 231, 235, 240, 249
porcupines 319
potatoes 147
potoos 143, 195
power stations 16
praying mantises 289
pregnancy (elephant) 289
prides 258, 263
primates 314–339
prisms 10
proboscis monkeys 336
pufferfish 248, 365
puffins 120, 170, 189
pumas 259, 265, 270
pupae 295
pups
  seals 307
  sharks 111
pushes and pulls 7
pylons 16
pythons 351

Q

Queen Alexandra's birdwing butterflies 206
quetzals 205
quiver trees 151

R

rabbits 153, 261, 265, 292
racing cars 24
radar 13
radio waves 13, 18, 19, 29
rafflesias 147, 201
railway signals 13
rain 84, 86, 88–89, 90, 139, 197
rainbows 10, 94
rainforests 87, 147, 153, 159, 194–219, 265, 272–273, 337
ramps 7
Random Access Memory (RAM) 21
rare animals 217
rattlesnakes 291, 346
rays 168, 231, 247
razorbills 170
razorshells 180
Read Only Memory (ROM) 21
rectum 51
recycling 31, 98, 99
red soldierfish 241

red uakaris 333
red-eyed tree frogs 213
redwoods, giant 138, 149
reef sharks 169, 231
reflexes 36
renewable energy 99
reserves, animal 265
retina 54
rhinos 308, 367
Richter Scale 77
ring-tailed lemurs 208, 209, 317
ringed plovers 172
rivers 80–81, 88, 178
rock doves 170
rock pools 106–107, 184–185
rocks 15, 66, 67, 73
rollercoasters 7
roots 134, 143, 155, 157, 186
rose petals 139
rubber 25

S

sabre-toothed cats 277
salamanders 367
salmon 81, 178
salt 125, 179
saltwater crocodiles 118
sand 175, 179, 180
sand dunes 171
sand hoppers 185
sand tiger sharks 111, 287
satellites 18
savannahs 268
scent-marking 269, 271
schools (fish) 108
scientists 26–27, 28, 29, 82, 98
scorpions 295, 347
sea anemones 106, 107, 183, 185, 236
sea cows 187
sea goldies 231
sea grasses 230
sea lions 111, 116
sea otters 117, 145
sea pinks 179
sea slugs 229
sea snakes 119
sea urchins 185, 230
seabirds 120–121, 123, 170, 171, 172–173, 176, 181, 189, 229, 303
seahorses 112, 227, 233, 235
seals 110, 116, 117, 165, 173, 307
seamounts 105

seashells 106, 166, 169, 177, 242
seashores 164–165, 174–175
seasons 96–97
seaweeds 124, 145, 151, 185, 227, 230, 233
see-saws 6
seedlings 137
seeds 140, 141, 149, 153, 155, 157, 158, 324
sensors 38, 39, 54, 55, 56
Serengeti, Africa 268
servals 262
setts 301
sharks 110–111, 169, 228, 231, 237, 245, 246, 287, 297, 359
sheep 153, 158
shingle 174
shrimps 180, 237
Siberian tigers 254, 255, 275
sifakas 331
silverbacks 332, 333
silvered langurs 330
singing 47, 115, 117
skateboards 38, 39

380

skating 79
skeleton 42–43
skin 38–39, 60
skipping 331
skyscrapers 12, 13
sleeping sickness 369
sloths 144, 198, 298
slow loris 325
slugs 207, 229
smartphones 23
smells 56–57
smiling 45
snails 207, 368
snakes 119, 209, 218, 303, 351, 357
  poisonous 291, 346, 357
snow 78, 90–91
snow leopards 274
snowflakes 78, 79, 90
sockets 16, 17
soda 25
soil 157
sounds 11, 55
spaghetti 149
speaking 59
spider monkeys 314, 327
spiderlings 297
spiders 126, 197, 297, 352, 364, 365
spiny lobsters 249
spireshells 177
spits 174

sponges 107, 185, 233
spring 96
squid 127, 237, 247
squirrel monkeys 319
squirrels 296
stacks 174
stalagmites and stalactites 85
starfish 106, 119, 185, 230, 238, 249
static electricity 17
steel 13, 14
stems 134, 137
stick insects 143
stings 228, 231, 236, 347, 349, 355
stomach 49, 51
stonefish 227, 348
strandline 181
stratus clouds 89
streams 80, 84
submarines 82
summer 96
Sun 66, 95, 96, 97, 137
sun bears 211
sun dogs (mock suns) 95
sundew plants 148
sunfish 109
sunlight 10, 94, 145
surfing 129
swallowing 49, 51
sweat 39

sweet potatoes 143
sweetlips 249

T

tadpoles 285
tails 315, 331
tamarins 329
tapirs 199
tarsiers 316
taste 56, 57
taste buds 57
teeth
  animal 203, 219, 277, 350, 353, 359
  egg tooth 301
  fangs 337, 346, 358, 364
  human 50–51
  tusks 115, 219, 349
temperatures 9, 90
tentacles 127, 183, 225, 235, 236, 239, 355, 363
termites 318
territories 263, 269, 271
thermometers 9
thinking 59

thresher sharks 111
thunderstorms 17, 92
tides 106, 165, 180, 181, 184
tiger beetles 171
tiger sharks 111
tigers 171, 214, 217, 254–255, 257, 260, 261, 263, 266, 267, 269, 272, 275, 277, 321
toads 181, 217
toadstools 141
toenails 41
toilet 51, 53, 61
tokay geckos 195
tongues
 animal 146, 217, 339
 human 49, 57
tool use, animal 318, 323
tornadoes 92
tortoises 273, 275
toucans 196
touch 38, 39, 59
tower shells 177
trains 7, 12, 13
tree frogs 213
tree houses 153
tree kangaroos 204

trees 138, 142, 150–151, 153, 154, 155, 186, 264, 271, 321, 324
trenches 83, 105
trilobites 72, 73
trunks (elephants) 287
tsetse flies 369
tsunamis 167
tube worms 126
tulips 149
turtles 119, 168, 188–189, 226, 230, 275, 289, 361
tusks 115, 219, 349
typhoons 93

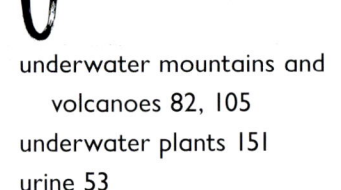

U

underwater mountains and volcanoes 82, 105
underwater plants 151
urine 53

V

vaccinations 61
vegetables 48, 159
veins 53
venom 228, 291, 347, 349, 363
Venus flytraps 156
vine snakes 209
vision
 animals 279, 316, 328
 humans 54

voicebox 47
volcanoes 71, 74, 75, 82, 85, 105

W

walruses 116, 117, 349
warrens 292
wasps 307, 349
waste, bodily 51, 53
water cycle 88
water vapour 88
waterfalls 80
waterskiing 129
waves 83, 167, 175
webs 365
whale sharks 245
whales 114–115, 284, 295, 345
wheat 149, 151
wheelbarrows 7
wheels 7
white light 10
whitetip reef sharks 231
wild cats 187
wildebeest 268, 350, 360
Wilson's storm petrels 121
wind turbines 99
windpipe 46